Library of Congress Cataloging-in-Publication Data

The Supreme Court of the United States:
   Its Beginnings & Its Justices 1790–1991
   p.   cm.
   Includes bibliographical references (p.   )
   1. United States. Supreme Court—Biography.
   2. United States. Supreme Court—History.
   I. Commission on the Bicentennial of the United
States Constitution

KF8744.S87 1992
347.73'26'09—dc20
[347.3073509]   92-10459
                CIP

Photographs printed with permission.

The Supreme Court

OF THE UNITED STATES

Its Beginnings & Its Justices 1790–1991

Commission on the Bicentennial of the United States Constitution

Contents

Preface

WILLIAM H. REHNQUIST
Chief Justice of the United States

THE DRAMATIC CHANGES which have occurred in eastern Europe at roughly the same time that we celebrate the Bicentennial of the Bill of Rights highlight the importance of our observance. The Framers of our Constitution bequeathed to posterity two new concepts in government. The first was the idea of a chief executive independent of the legislative branch, and the second was the idea of an independent constitutional court with the power of judicial review. The first of these ideas has found little favor outside of the United States. But the second — the constitutional court — has been more and more widely copied during the twentieth century, first in western Europe and elsewhere, and now in eastern Europe. Judged by its popularity in other countries, the concept of an independent Supreme Court with the authority to declare legislative acts unconstitutional must be reckoned as the major contribution of the United States to the art of government. The belief in a court which has the authority to keep the government within bounds set by a written constitution has had worldwide appeal. ∞ The Supreme Court of the United States, of course, did not "spring full blown from the head of Zeus" or anyone else. What Justice Holmes said of our government as a whole applies equally to it. The words of the Constitution "called into life a being the development of which could not have been foreseen by the most gifted of its begetters." The present day position of prestige and authority occupied by the Supreme Court has gradually developed over a period of two centuries, developed because of the way the Justices of that Court throughout this period have exercised the judicial power which they were granted by the Constitution. This book is composed of biographical sketches of each of the one hundred and six Justices of the Court, material which is most useful to anyone who seeks to understand the Supreme Court and the part that it has played in our history. ∞

Foreword

WARREN E. BURGER

Chairman of the Commission on the Bicentennial of the United States Constitution 1985–1992
Chief Justice of the United States 1969–1986

ONE HUNDRED AND SIX JUSTICES have served on the bench of the Supreme Court of the United States since February 2, 1790, when the Court first met. The names of some of the early Justices are familiar — John Jay, John Marshall, Joseph Story, John Marshall Harlan. Other Justices who served early in this century come to mind readily: William Howard Taft, who served first as President and then as Chief Justice, Oliver Wendell Holmes, Jr., and Charles Evans Hughes. Still others are scarcely household names, yet collectively they have exercised a profound influence on American life. No single book could tell the full story of the Court or its Justices. This book is intended as a beginning — an appetizer — rather than a definitive treatment of their lives. In preparing this book, our aim has been to present the basic facts of the life of each Justice in a form useful for teachers, students, and the general public. This book is also intended as a tribute to all of the Justices who have served on the Supreme Court, and will, we hope, be an inspiration to others to pursue further study of "this Honorable Court." ∞ Most Americans are only vaguely acquainted with the story of the Supreme Court. In recent years, the opening of the annual Term of the Supreme Court on the first Monday in October has become an increasingly well-publicized event. Newspaper and broadcast commentators discuss cases that have been set for argument during the Term and speculate about possible outcomes. As the Term progresses, the announcement of a major decision is often headline news. Relatively few people, however, are familiar with the Court's early history. The following pages sketch some of the more significant aspects of the Supreme Court's early years, including the origins of the Federal Judiciary, the practice of circuit riding, and the emergence of the Court as a co-equal branch of government under the "Great Chief Justice," John Marshall.

ALTHOUGH PRESIDENT GEORGE WASHINGTON viewed the Federal Judiciary "as the chief-Pillar upon which our national Government must rest," it would have been hard to predict the Supreme Court's future from its humble origins in the federal Constitutional Convention held in Philadelphia in 1787. The Framers of the Constitution recognized the flaws in the Articles of Confederation: among other things, although the Articles provided for a Continental Congress, the Congress had no Executive to execute its laws, and no Judiciary to construe them. Accordingly, the Framers decided to create a national government that consisted of three independent branches: a Legislative Branch, an Executive Branch, and — of particular interest here — a Judicial Branch. Interestingly, however, the Framers did not spend nearly as much time at the Constitutional Convention debating the subject of the Judicial Branch as they did on the Legislative and the Executive Branches.

The Constitution provided for "one supreme Court," set forth basic guidelines on what kinds of cases federal courts could hear, and gave the President authority to appoint federal judges "by and with the Advice and Consent of the Senate." The Framers were strongly concerned with preserving judicial independence, so they granted federal judges permanent tenure "during good Behaviour" and prohibited any reduction in their compensation in order to ensure that neither Congress nor the Executive could exercise direct control over the Judiciary. Beyond these basic principles, most questions concerning the form and structure of the Judiciary were left for later resolution by Congress. Thus, Congress had to establish by legislation such details as how many members the Supreme Court would have, what other federal courts would be created, and, within the limits set forth in the Constitution, what kinds of cases those courts would have the authority to decide.

On September 24, 1789, five months after President George Washington took office, the Judiciary Act of 1789 became law. The Judiciary Act was drafted largely by Senator Oliver Ellsworth, who was later to serve as the third Chief Justice. In addition to establishing the Supreme Court, the Act divided the country into three circuits, Eastern, Middle, and Southern, and established three Circuit Courts. Significantly, the Act did not provide separate judgeships for the Circuit Courts, but directed that each Circuit Court was to consist of two Supreme Court Justices and one District Judge. The Act also established thirteen District Courts and thirteen District Court judgeships, providing at least one District Court for each state then in the Union. Under the framework established by the Act, the District Courts functioned as trial courts, the Circuit Courts heard appeals from the District Courts and also served as trial courts for certain kinds of cases, and the Supreme Court was the highest appellate court, with jurisdiction to review appeals from both District and Circuit Courts. The court system established by the Judiciary Act can be thus likened to a pyramid, with the District Courts at the base, the Circuit Courts forming the middle, and the Supreme Court at the apex.

The Judiciary Act provided for a six-member Supreme Court with a Chief Justice and five Associate Justices, thus formally establishing the titles of "Chief Justice" and "Associate Justice." Interestingly, in Article III there is no mention of a "Chief Justice" or "Associate Justices" — only "Judges." The sole reference in the Constitution to the office of Chief Justice is found in Article I, Section 3, which provides that if a President is impeached, "the Chief Justice shall preside" over the Senate trial. Thus, separation of powers considerations notwithstanding, the Constitution requires that the highest judicial officer in the nation preside over sessions of the Senate on an impeachment trial of the Chief Executive. Such a trial has been held only once in our history, when Chief Justice Salmon P. Chase presided over the impeachment trial and ultimate acquittal of President Andrew Johnson in 1868.

On February 1, 1790, the Supreme Court met for the first time in an "uncommonly crowded" courtroom at the Royal Exchange Building in New York City. Present were Chief Justice John Jay and Justices James Wilson and William Cushing. Because only three Justices were present, the Court adjourned to February 2, when Justice John Blair arrived. Although Justice Robert Harrison attempted to attend the session, he fell ill en route from Maryland, and was forced to resign his commission on account of poor health. Justice John Rutledge was also unable to attend the first session of the Supreme Court and resigned from the Court in 1791 to accept an appointment as Chief Justice of the South Carolina Court of Common Pleas. With no cases yet on the docket, the Justices spent the first session attending to such administrative matters as the appointment of the Court Clerk, the adoption of Rules of Court, and the admission of attorneys to the Supreme Court Bar.

During the first years of the Supreme Court, the Justices wore ornate scarlet-faced robes trimmed with gold piping; some of the Justices also wore wigs. This attire was soon dropped, probably because it reminded people of the "undemocratic" traditions that the country had recently fought so hard to reject. According to one account, Thomas Jefferson "was against any needless official apparel," and urged that the Justices "discard the monstrous wig which makes the English Judges look like rats peeping through bunches of oakum!" By the time that John Marshall became Chief Justice in 1801, the scarlet-colored robes had been abandoned in favor of simpler black robes and the Justices had also abandoned the wigs.

Once the Judicial Branch was established and functioning, it remained to be seen whether it would prove to be a truly co-equal branch of government. During the first decade of the Court, the Justices devoted most of their time to organizing the federal judicial system and riding circuit to hear cases as trial and appellate judges. It took time for the concept of "one supreme Court" with a national role to be realized. Prior to 1790, the only courts in existence had been state courts, and many state court judges and lawyers were initially reluctant to accept the new federal judicial order. Moreover, the District and Circuit Courts created by Congress were courts of limited jurisdiction, and in the early years of the Republic their work consisted largely of admiralty cases and commercial disputes between citizens of different states. Controversies that implicated the national government and its laws gradually made their way into the federal court system. As a result, the Supreme Court wrote fewer than 70 opinions in its first decade, from its first session in 1790 to the end of 1800 — approximately one-half of the annual output of the Supreme Court in recent years.

THE JUSTICES' CIRCUIT-RIDING DUTIES as federal trial and appellate judges were for many years more burdensome than their work on the Supreme Court. Although circuit riding played an important role in educating citizens far removed from the nation's capital about the federal government, on balance the burdens that circuit riding placed on the Justices far outweighed its public benefits. Circuit riding also dissuaded many prominent lawyers and state judges from accepting appointments to the Supreme Court.

The appearance of a Supreme Court Justice on circuit was an important event. The Justices used the occasion to explain the new federal government, particularly when they met with grand juries. The "charges" or instructions given by the Justices often included informal "civics lessons" unrelated to the merits of any case: the Justices made appeals to patriotism, honor, and duty, and explained the role of the federal government and the concept of federalism.

They were well aware of the tensions between different states that arose out of their diverse colonial origins and ongoing disputes over territorial boundaries and trade and commerce. The Articles of Confederation had been more like a multilateral treaty among sovereign states than a document constituting a nation and, although it may seem strange to us now, the concept of the "United States" was still relatively new in 1790. In the words of one historian, "the Constitution, as far as nationality was concerned, was no more than a promissory note," and "the struggle to establish the power of the federal government would rage intensively, but intermittently, from the rebellions and resolutions of the 1790s through the middle of the nineteenth century." In the nation's formative years, circuit-riding probably helped in some measure to ease public concern about the new federal government.

A serious defect in the circuit-riding system was that the Justices were required to sit on circuit court cases that were subsequently appealed to the Supreme Court, putting them in the awkward position of taking part in reviewing their own decisions. The Justices had pointed out early to President Washington and Congress the incompatibility of having Justices of the Supreme Court sitting in review of cases that they may have heard on an appeal on circuit. On occasion, a Justice would have to recuse himself when a case that he had heard on circuit came before the Supreme Court.

Although circuit riding was not entirely without its rewards, the burden of meeting twice in a year in Supreme Court sessions and traveling circuit took a heavy toll on the Justices, and sometimes made it difficult for President Washington to find qualified candidates who were willing to serve on the Court. In letters to family and friends, the Justices recorded the difficulties of circuit riding. For Justices who had to ride circuit by horseback, stagecoach, and, later, steamboat, travel was arduous and often physically debilitating.

The Justices journeyed long distances over crude and poorly marked roads and lodged at taverns and public houses that were often crowded, dirty, and uncomfortable, leading one observer to remark that, in America, "a Junior Judge must lead . . . the life of a Post Boy." Even when the Justices were offered more comfortable lodgings by private citizens, they sometimes felt compelled to decline them for fear that to do otherwise would raise questions about their impartiality. For example, although Chief Justice Jay was offered the hospitality of friends and well-wishers while traveling the Eastern Circuit, he made it a policy to decline such invitations, especially from lawyers, despite his desire for a clean room and good food. On one occasion he answered an invitation: "As a man, and as your friend, I should be happy in accepting [your friendly invitation]; but, as a judge, I have my doubts."

The Justices were also subject to whatever perils faced the population at large in the regions that they traveled. There were real hazards in traveling during periods of inclement weather and seasonal flooding. Justice James Iredell was not only robbed while riding circuit, but also suffered a violent carriage accident when a horse bolted and ran his carriage into a tree. Moreover, in the days before sanitary water works, diseases often spread unchecked. In 1793, a yellow fever epidemic forced an early termination of the Supreme Court's August session in Philadelphia.

Justice Iredell was a committed and vocal opponent of the circuit-riding system that had been established by Congress. Riding the enormous Southern Circuit in May and June of 1790, he wrote, "I scarcely thought there had been so much barren land in all America as I have passed through." On February 11, 1791, Justice Iredell wrote Chief Justice Jay and Associate Justices William Cushing and James Wilson to protest his reassignment to the Southern Circuit; he had ridden 1,900 miles in 1790, a great deal of travel in that day. Chief Justice Jay replied that "[t]he circuits press upon us all; and your share of the task has hitherto been no more than in due proportion," but Justice Iredell was not content to let the issue rest there and, on January 17, 1792, he wrote again to Chief Justice Jay to protest that he could "no longer undertake so very unequal a proportion of duty" in riding the Southern Circuit. Although the Justices considered forgoing $500 of their $3,500 annual salary if their circuit riding duties were eliminated, Chief Justice Jay advised Iredell that only an Act of Congress could rescue them from the ordeal. In the Fall of 1792, Justice Iredell secured a transfer to the Eastern Circuit. He praised New England for its "regularity and decency" but commented that "[t]here are the most stones in [the land] I ever saw." In August 1794, Justice Iredell refused to ride the Southern Circuit in Justice Wilson's place, explaining that he had already covered the circuit five times in four years.

Justice Iredell's complaints were well-taken, and he was not alone in voicing displeasure with the onerous task of riding circuit. Other Justices were heard to complain that circuit riding required "perpetual Itineration," that it foreclosed any "Opportunity of consulting books, or of studying to advantage," and that circuit-riding duty had "taken me from my

Family half the year." As late as the 1840s, Justice Levi Woodbury wrote his wife:

> "The 'villainous' sea-sickness, which generally afflicts me in a Stage [coach] has yielded, in some degree, to my suffering from the extreme cold . . . . I think I never again, at this season of the year, will attempt this mode of journeying. Beside the evils before mentioned I have been elbowed by old women — jammed by young ones — suffocated by cigar smoke — sickened by the vapors of bitters and wiskey — my head knocked through the carriage top by careless drivers and my toes trodden to a jelly by unheeding passengers."

Not surprisingly, circuit riding had the potential to cause family difficulties. On one occasion, Justice Woodbury arrived home after a long ride on circuit to find his house empty. His wife, uncertain when the Justice would return, had decided to take a vacation without him. "Why do you talk of regret at my necessary absence on the Circuit to support my family and object to my going to Washington," he complained to her, yet "are still so unwilling to stay with me when at home?"

AS EARLY AS 1790, the Justices of the Supreme Court urged that they be freed from the burdens of circuit riding. President George Washington shared the view that the Justices should be granted "relief from these disagreeable [circuit] tours," but Congress was slow to take action.

In 1792, the Justices unanimously joined in writing to President Washington "in strong and explicit terms":

> "[W]e cannot reconcile ourselves to the idea of existing in exile from our families, and of being subjected to a kind of life, on which we cannot reflect, without experiencing sensations and emotions, more easy to conceive than proper for us to express."

In their letter to President Washington, the Justices enclosed a letter to the Congress, stating in no uncertain terms:

> "[T]he task of holding twenty seven circuit Courts a year, in the different States, from New Hampshire to Georgia, besides two Sessions of the Supreme Court at Philadelphia, in the two most severe seasons of the year, is a task which considering the extent of the United States, and the small number of Judges, is too burdensome . . . .

[S]ome of the present Judges do not enjoy health and strength of body suffi-
cient to enable them to undergo the toilsome Journies through different cli-
mates and seasons, which they are called upon to undertake; nor is it probable
that any set of Judges however robust, would be able to support and punctually
execute such severe duties for any length of time."

The President transmitted the Justices' complaint to Congress and, in 1793, Congress responded
by passing an act that lightened — but did not eliminate — the Justices' circuit-riding responsi-
bilities by changing the number of Supreme Court Justices who were required to sit on the
Circuit Courts from two to one.

In practical effect, since there were at that time six Supreme Court Justices and three
Circuit Courts that each met twice annually, the 1793 Act permitted the Justices to ride circuit
only once a year instead of twice. The relief provided by the 1793 Act was short-lived, however,
because the caseload of both the Supreme Court and the Circuit Courts steadily increased. In
1801 Congress increased the number of Circuit Courts from three to six, and in 1807 a seventh
Circuit Court was established. Because of the continuing difficulties with the circuit-riding
system, Chief Justice Jay wrote to Senator Rufus King in December 1793, and all of the Justices
wrote again to President Washington in February 1794, but no further relief was had during
Jay's tenure.

A significant effort to reform the circuit-riding system fell victim to partisan politics. In
the election of 1800, Federalist President John Adams lost to Anti-Federalist Republican candidate Thomas Jefferson, and control of the Congress shifted from the Federalists to the Anti-
Federalists. On February 13, 1801 — approximately one month before the victors of the election
of 1800 were sworn into office — an Act was passed which created sixteen judgeships for the
Circuit Courts and abolished all circuit riding. The Jeffersonians quickly labeled the "Midnight
Judges Act" a wasteful attempt by President Adams and the defeated Federalists to appoint
judges of their own political inclination to the federal bench before they left office. On March 8,
1802, the "Midnight Judges Act" was repealed, and circuit riding continued.

At this point, the Justices considered reviving a constitutional argument against circuit
riding that had first been made by the original Justices of the Supreme Court in 1790. Article III of
the Constitution granted the Supreme Court original jurisdiction over certain kinds of cases, but

further provided that "[i]n all the other Cases, . . . the Supreme Court shall have appellate Jurisdiction . . . with such Exceptions, and under such Regulations as the Congress shall make." Like the Jay Court before it, the Marshall Court contemplated arguing that the constitutional requirement that the Supreme Court exercise limited "appellate jurisdiction" should be read as prohibiting them from being required to sit as judges on lower federal courts. This argument was ultimately rejected, however, when the case of *Stuart* v. *Laird* reached the Supreme Court in 1803. In that case, the Court upheld the constitutionality of the legislation repealing the "Midnight Judges" Act of 1801, reasoning that the practice of the original Justices of the Supreme Court to ride circuit furnished "a contemporary [constitutional] interpretation of the most forcible nature."

Further reforms in the circuit-riding system took place gradually over an extended period of time. The piecemeal nature of these reforms can be attributed to a mix of Congressional indifference and animosity towards the Judiciary, the failure of lawmakers to understand the requirements of sound judicial administration and, perhaps, Congressional preoccupation with other issues. Some Members of Congress recognized the senseless burden that circuit riding placed on the Justices; for example, in response to the argument that circuit riding rendered the Justices better able "to acquire a competent knowledge of local institutions," Pennsylvania Senator Gouverneur Morris — who had been one of the leading delegates to the Constitutional Convention in 1787 — remarked in 1802:

> "I am not quite convinced that riding rapidly from one end of this country to
> another is the best way to study law. I am inclined to believe that knowledge
> may be more conveniently acquired in the closet than in the high road."

The prevailing view, however, was expressed by South Carolina Senator William Smith, who insisted that if the Justices were allowed to linger in the nation's capital they would become "completely cloistered within the City of Washington, and their decisions, instead of emanating from enlarged and liberalized minds, will assume a severe and local character." The worthy Senator perhaps did not anticipate a time like the present, when the Congress itself spends most of the year in session in Washington.

Shortly after the repeal of the "Midnight Judges Act" in 1802, the circuit-riding system was modified so that a Circuit Court could be held by a single District Judge. By permitting circuit sessions to be held by one judge, this modification eliminated the need for even one

Supreme Court Justice to sit on every circuit. In 1844, as the Supreme Court fell further and further behind in its caseload, the Justices were relieved from attending "more than one term of the circuit court within any district of such circuit in any one year." In 1869, Congress created nine new judgeships for the Circuit Courts and reduced the required attendance by Supreme Court Justices to one session every two years. Finally, in 1891, one hundred years after the Justices and President Washington had expressed concern about the "burdensome" task of circuit riding, the Circuit Court of Appeals Act was passed, establishing nine Circuit Courts of Appeals with permanent judgeships. Although the 1891 Act permitted Supreme Court Justices to sit as Circuit Judges, it did not require them to do so.

AFTER CHIEF JUSTICE John Marshall was appointed by President John Adams in January 1801, the Supreme Court began to shape the fundamental legal principles — the foundation blocks — upon which our constitutional system of government has rested for nearly 200 years. The Marshall Court's 1803 decision in *Marbury* v. *Madison* pointedly confirmed the Supreme Court's power, implicit in Article III of the Constitution, to "say what the law is" and to invalidate a legislative or executive act that is contrary to the Constitution.

Although the significance of *Marbury* was that it declared an Act of Congress unconstitutional, and thus established the Supreme Court's role in relation to the political branches of the federal government, the principle of judicial review itself was not new. For example, in 1795, in *Van Horne's Lessee* v. *Dorrance*, Justice Paterson explained that, in the American experience,

> "[A] Constitution is the sun of the political system, around which all Legislative, Executive, and Judicial bodies must revolve. Whatever may be the case in other countries, yet in this there can be no doubt, that every act of the Legislature, repugnant to the Constitution, is absolutely void."

The principle advanced by Justice Paterson in *Van Horne's Lessee* was reiterated the following year in *Ware* v. *Hylton*, when the Supreme Court invoked the Treaty Clause in the Constitution to strike down a Virginia statute on the ground that it conflicted with the 1783 Treaty of Peace between the United States and Great Britain.

Notwithstanding these precedents, the Supreme Court's decision in *Marbury* aroused Thomas Jefferson's latent hostility toward the Judiciary. Jefferson was essentially a parliamentarian, and he resented the idea that the Judicial Branch could check the political branches by declaring their actions unconstitutional. Moreover, because the Judicial Branch was staffed almost exclusively with men appointed by Washington and Adams, Jefferson considered it a stronghold of "Federalist troublemakers." Jefferson's views were aptly expressed by his close friend, Virginia Congressman William Branch Giles, who was a leading Anti-Federalist in the House of Representatives. Shortly after Jefferson's Inaugural in 1801, Giles wrote Jefferson: "It appears to me that the only check upon the judiciary system as it is now organized and filled is the removal of all its [judges] indiscriminately."

Perhaps emboldened by the successful repeal of the "Midnight Judges Act" in 1802, Jefferson launched a campaign of intimidation calculated to curtail the independence of the Judicial Branch. In 1803, Jefferson sent a collection of documents to the House of Representatives for the purpose of impeaching New Hampshire District Judge John Pickering. Pickering, who was senile and alcoholic, had not been performing his judicial duties. Enfeebled as he was, Pickering did not appear either in person or by counsel at his Senate trial, and the Senate removed him in short order in 1804.

Jefferson next turned his attention to Supreme Court Justice Samuel Chase of Maryland, the only Supreme Court Justice who has ever been subjected to an impeachment trial. Chase, an arch-Federalist, was despised in Jeffersonian circles because he had personally lobbied for passage of the Alien and Sedition Acts of 1798. Following his Senate trial in 1805, however, Chase was acquitted by a narrow margin. Chase was represented by exceptionally able lawyers who were as interested in repelling Jefferson's attack on the Judicial Branch as they were in saving Chase himself. At least among Federalists, there was a general feeling that the impeachment of Chase was only "the entering wedge to the compleat annihilation of our wise and independant Judiciary."

The Senate's failure to convict Chase signaled an end to Jefferson's concerted efforts to rein in the Judicial Branch, but Jefferson and his followers continued to make scattered attacks on the Judiciary well into the nineteenth century. For example, in the early 1820s, Jefferson wrote to Justice William Johnson complaining about the Supreme Court's practice — instituted by Chief Justice Marshall in 1801 — of announcing decisions of the Court in a single written opinion rather than in individual opinions signed by each of the Justices:

"The practice [of issuing a single opinion] is certainly convenient for the lazy, the modest & the incompetent. It saves them the trouble of developing their opinion methodically and even of making up an opinion at all. That of seriatim argument shews whether every judge has taken the trouble of understanding the case, of investigating it minutely, and of forming an opinion for himself, instead of pinning it on another's sleeve."

Jefferson's complaint about Chief Justice Marshall's approach to opinion-writing was but one of many complaints that he voiced about the Chief Justice during Marshall's long tenure in office.

From the time that *Marbury* was decided in 1803 until the Jeffersonian attack on the Judicial Branch subsided in 1805, Chief Justice Marshall generally distanced himself from the political controversy over judicial power and judicial independence. Although Marshall was initially interested in challenging the Jeffersonians' repeal of the "Midnight Judges" Act on constitutional grounds, he ultimately denied a challenge to the Act's constitutionality while presiding on the Circuit Court of Appeals, and his ruling was affirmed in Justice Paterson's opinion for the Court in *Stuart* v. *Laird*. In a letter to Justice Chase in 1804, Marshall — who was at that time still apprehensive about Jefferson's hostility towards the Judiciary — surprisingly expressed the view that it might be preferable to give Congress the power to review decisions of the Supreme Court than to permit Congress to impeach judges on the basis that it disagreed with their views:

"I think the modern doctrine of impeachment should yield to an appellate jurisdiction in the legislature. A reversal of those legal opinions deemed unsound by the legislature would certainly better comport with the mildness of our character than [would] a removal of the judge who has rendered them unknowing of his fault."

It may be that Marshall offered this suggestion as a "bargaining chip" to blunt or defuse the Anti-Federalist attack until more support developed for the Court. In any event, it was an uncharacteristic expression from a man who had long championed the concept of an independent judiciary.

After surviving the Jeffersonian challenge to the Court's independence, however, Marshall turned once again to the task of firmly defining the national government's constitutional powers in relation to the states. In *Dartmouth College* v. *Woodward* in 1819, Marshall, writing for the Court, ruled that the New Hampshire Legislature's attempt to modify the colonial charter of

Dartmouth College and subject the College to state control violated the constitutional command that "[n]o State shall . . . pass any . . . Law impairing the Obligation of Contracts." In that same year, Marshall's opinion for the Court in *McCulloch* v. *Maryland* upheld the constitutionality of the Second Bank of the United States, which had been created by Act of Congress in 1816, on the basis of the implied powers of Congress under the Constitution. Marshall's opinion also invalidated Maryland's efforts to impose an indirect tax on the Bank as a federal instrumentality. *McCulloch* clarified the relationship between federal and state governments by establishing not only that the federal government could exercise constitutional powers that were implicit and not express, but that, within its sphere of authority, the federal government was supreme. In *Gibbons* v. *Ogden*, the Court rejected arguments that the State of New York had the power to grant a steamship company an exclusive license to conduct trade on the navigable waters within the State. *Gibbons* confirmed Congress's power to regulate interstate transportation under the Commerce Clause, and helped to implement the Framers' unarticulated vision of the United States as a "common market." Marshall had no difficulty in deciding that "interstate commerce" included "interstate transportation." The *Gibbons* holding was another victory for judicial independence.

Despite failing health, Chief Justice Marshall did not resign from the bench but died in office in 1835. Marshall may have believed that he could outlive President Andrew Jackson's second term in office, which ended in 1837. Had Marshall survived, he would have denied Jackson — who, like Thomas Jefferson, was a believer in states' rights and no friend of the Supreme Court — the privilege of appointing the next Chief Justice.

In his passing, Marshall left behind a rich and unparalleled legacy with lasting implications for the shape of American government. Under his stewardship, the Supreme Court survived potentially fatal attacks on its independence, confirmed the power of judicial review, confirmed the supremacy of the national government, and facilitated the success of the American political experiment by recognizing broad powers in Congress to enact laws pursuant to its express as well as its implied powers. The history of the Marshall Court, however, was merely the prologue to an important and, at times, turbulent history that has been marked by watershed decisions and political debate over the Supreme Court's proper role in the constitutional order.

Like all of our governmental institutions, the character and quality of the work of the Supreme Court depends upon the people who serve on it. While the vast majority of the Court's decisions have met with popular acceptance and approval and withstood the test of time, the Court has also, on occasion, committed grievous errors. To appreciate this fact, one need not look beyond the Court's pernicious 1857 decision in *Dred Scott* v. *Sandford*, where the Court ruled that a slave was property and could not be a citizen, and invalidated the Missouri Compromise of 1820 by declaring that Congress could not constitutionally outlaw slavery in the territories. In purporting to resolve the divisive issue of slavery by judicial decree and invalidating an Act of Congress for the first time since *Marbury* was decided in 1803, the *Dred Scott* decision generated enormous controversy while making further political compromise impossible and, in the view of many historians, helped to accelerate the outbreak of the Civil War. In the wake of the *Dred Scott* decision, the Supreme Court's prestige and standing reached its lowest ebb.

Following the Civil War and the adoption of the Thirteenth, Fourteenth, and Fifteenth Amendments, the Supreme Court made another major misstep when, in 1896, in *Plessy* v. *Ferguson*, it rejected a constitutional challenge to state laws that mandated segregation by requiring "separate but equal" public facilities and accommodations for whites and blacks. The error of *Plessy* was not fully corrected until 1954 when, in *Brown* v. *Board of Education*, the Supreme Court ruled that "in the field of public education the doctrine of 'separate but equal' has no place." The *Brown* decision reflected a shift in popular opinion of more enlightened times, and gave significant impetus to the civil rights movement of the 1950s and 1960s, which ultimately succeeded in eradicating state-sponsored segregation throughout the nation.

The Supreme Court has also periodically been the object of political assaults of varying intensity. For example, in 1937, in a political maneuver that was reminiscent of Jefferson's attempt to curtail the independence of the Judiciary in the early nineteenth century, President Franklin Roosevelt proposed what came to be known as his "Court-packing plan." Frustrated with the Supreme Court's disapproval of various New Deal programs on constitutional grounds, President Roosevelt asked Congress to enact legislation giving him the authority to appoint an additional Justice to the Court for every sitting Justice over the age of 70. To justify his proposal, Roosevelt attempted to create the impression that Members of the Court were having difficulty handling the Court's caseload because of their advanced age. Had Roosevelt succeeded, he would have been authorized to appoint six new Justices to the Court, ensuring a majority that would likely support his legislative agenda. As events unfolded, however, President Roosevelt gained another seat on the Court with the retirement of Justice Van Devanter, and Congress roundly rejected the President's legislative proposal.

As we stand on the brink of the twenty-first century, the Supreme Court's place in the framework of our constitutional democracy seems secure. Justice Joseph Story, echoing what young John Marshall put to Patrick Henry at the Virginia Ratification Debates in 1788, wrote:

> "Where there is no judicial department to interpret, pronounce, and execute the law, to decide controversies, and to enforce rights, the government must either perish by its own imbecility, or the other departments of government must usurp powers, for the purpose of commanding obedience, to the destruction of liberty . . . . In every well organized government, therefore, with reference to the security of both public rights and private rights, it is indispensable, that there should be a judicial department to ascertain, and decide rights, to punish crimes, to administer justice, and to protect the innocent from injury and usurpation."

Americans have an instinctive sense of the importance of an independent Judiciary to the liberties that we hold dear and, although the independence of the Supreme Court may well be challenged in the future, there is every reason to believe that the Court will endure.

THE JUDICIAL POWER OF THE UNITED STATES,

SHALL BE VESTED IN ONE SUPREME COURT,

AND IN SUCH INFERIOR COURTS

AS THE CONGRESS MAY FROM TIME TO TIME

ORDAIN AND ESTABLISH.

CONSTITUTION, ARTICLE III, SECTION I

CHIEF JUSTICES

of the United States 1789 – 1991

JOHN JAY

Chief Justice 1789 – 1795

JOHN JAY was born on December 12, 1745, in New York, New York, and grew up in Rye, New York. He was graduated from King's College (now Columbia University) in 1764. He read law in a New York law firm and was admitted to the bar in 1768. ∞ Jay served as a delegate to both the First and Second Continental Congresses, and was elected President of the Continental Congress in 1778. He also served in the New York State militia. In 1779, Jay was sent on a diplomatic mission to Spain in an effort to gain recognition and economic assistance for the United States. In 1783, he helped to negotiate the Treaty of Paris, which marked the end of the Revolutionary War. Jay favored a stronger union and contributed five essays to *The Federalist Papers* in support of the new Constitution. ∞ President George Washington nominated Jay the first Chief Justice of the United States on September 24, 1789. The Senate confirmed the appointment on September 26, 1789. ∞ In April 1794, Jay negotiated a treaty with Great Britain, which became known as the Jay Treaty. After serving as Chief Justice for five years, Jay resigned from the Supreme Court on June 29, 1795, and became Governor of New York. He declined a second appointment as Chief Justice in 1800, and President John Adams then nominated John Marshall for the position. Jay died on May 17, 1829, at the age of eighty-three. ∞

JOHN RUTLEDGE

Chief Justice 1795 ∞ *Associate Justice 1790 – 1791*

JOHN RUTLEDGE was born in Charleston, South Carolina, in September 1739. He studied law at the Inns of Court in England, and was admitted to the English bar in 1760. ∞ In 1761, Rutledge was elected to the South Carolina Commons House of Assembly. In 1764, he was appointed Attorney General of South Carolina by the King's Governor and served for ten months. Rutledge served as the youngest delegate to the Stamp Act Congress of 1765, which petitioned King George III for repeal of the Act. ∞ Rutledge headed the South Carolina delegation to the Constitutional Convention in 1787 and served as a member of the South Carolina Ratification Convention the following year. ∞ On September 24, 1789, President George Washington nominated Rutledge one of the original Associate Justices of the Supreme Court of the United States. The Senate confirmed the appointment two days later. After one year on the Supreme Court, Rutledge resigned in 1791 to become Chief Justice of South Carolina's highest court. ∞ On August 12, 1795, President George Washington nominated Rutledge Chief Justice of the United States. He served in that position as a recess appointee for four months, but the Senate refused to confirm him. Rutledge died on June 21, 1800, at the age of sixty. ∞

OLIVER ELLSWORTH

Chief Justice 1796 – 1800

OLIVER ELLSWORTH was born on April 29, 1745, in Windsor, Connecticut. Ellsworth attended Yale College until the end of his sophomore year, and then transferred to the College of New Jersey (now Princeton University), where he was graduated in 1766. He read law in a law office for four years and was admitted to the bar in 1779. ∞ Ellsworth was a member of the Connecticut General Assembly from 1773 to 1776. From 1777 to 1784, he served as a delegate to the Continental Congress and worked on many of its committees. After service on the Connecticut Council of Safety and the Governor's Council, he became a Judge of the Superior Court of Connecticut in 1785. ∞ As a delegate to the Federal Constitutional Convention in Philadelphia in 1787, Ellsworth helped formulate the "Connecticut Compromise," which resolved a critical debate between the large and small states over representation in Congress. ∞ Ellsworth was elected to the First Federal Congress as a Senator. There he chaired the committee that drafted the Judiciary Act of 1789, which established the federal court system. ∞ On March 3, 1796, President George Washington nominated Ellsworth Chief Justice of the United States, and the Senate confirmed the appointment the following day. He resigned from the Supreme Court on September 30, 1800. Ellsworth died on November 26, 1807, at the age of sixty-two. ∞

JOHN MARSHALL

Chief Justice 1801 – 1835

JOHN MARSHALL was born on September 24, 1755, in Germantown, Virginia. Following service in the Revolutionary War, he attended a course of law lectures conducted by George Wythe at the College of William and Mary and continued the private study of law until his admission to practice in 1780. ∞ Marshall was elected to the Virginia House of Delegates in 1782, 1787, and 1795. In 1797, he accepted appointment as one of three envoys sent on a diplomatic mission to France. Although offered appointment to the United States Supreme Court in 1798, Marshall preferred to remain in private practice. ∞ Marshall was elected to the United States House of Representatives in 1799, and in 1800 was appointed Secretary of State by President John Adams. The following year, President Adams nominated Marshall Chief Justice of the United States, and the Senate confirmed the appointment on January 27, 1801. Notwithstanding his appointment as Chief Justice, Marshall continued to serve as Secretary of State throughout President Adams' term and, at President Thomas Jefferson's request, he remained in that office briefly following Jefferson's inauguration. Marshall served as Chief Justice for 34 years, the longest tenure of any Chief Justice. During his tenure, he helped establish the Supreme Court as the final authority on the meaning of the Constitution. Marshall died on July 6, 1835, at the age of seventy-nine. ∞

ROGER BROOKE TANEY

Chief Justice 1836 – 1864

ROGER BROOKE TANEY was born in Calvert County, Maryland, on March 17, 1777. He was graduated from Dickinson College in 1795. After reading law in a law office in Annapolis, Maryland, he was admitted to the bar in 1799. In the same year, he was elected to the Maryland House of Delegates. ∞ Defeated for re-election, Taney moved to Frederick, Maryland, and entered the practice of law. He was elected to the State Senate in 1816 and served until 1821. In 1823, Taney moved to Baltimore, where he continued the practice of law. From 1827 to 1831, Taney served as Attorney General for the State of Maryland. ∞ In 1831, Taney was appointed Attorney General of the United States by President Andrew Jackson. On September 23, 1833, Taney received a recess appointment as Secretary of the Treasury. When the recess appointment terminated, Taney was formally nominated to serve in that position, but the Senate declined to confirm the appointment in 1834. ∞ In 1835, Taney was nominated as Associate Justice by President Jackson to succeed Justice Duvall, but the Senate failed to confirm him. On December 28, 1835, President Jackson nominated Taney Chief Justice of the United States. The Senate confirmed the appointment on March 15, 1836. Taney served as Chief Justice for twenty-eight years, the second longest tenure of any Chief Justice, and died on October 12, 1864, at the age of eighty-seven. ∞

SALMON PORTLAND CHASE
Chief Justice 1864 – 1873

ALMON PORTLAND CHASE was born in Cornish, New Hampshire, on January 13, 1808, and was raised in Ohio. He returned to New Hampshire to attend Dartmouth College and was graduated in 1826 at the age of eighteen. He then moved to Washington, D.C., where he read law under Attorney General William Wirt. ∽ Chase was admitted to the bar in 1829 and moved to Cincinnati, Ohio, where he worked as a lecturer, writer, and editor while he established a legal practice. ∽ Chase became involved in the anti-slavery movement, and in 1848 he helped to write the platform of the Free Soilers Party. In 1848, the Ohio legislature elected Chase to the United States Senate, where he served one six-year term. In 1855, he was elected to a four-year term as Governor of Ohio, and in 1860 he was re-elected to the United States Senate. ∽ Chase resigned his Senate seat after only two days to accept a wartime appointment by President Abraham Lincoln as Secretary of the Treasury. He resigned from that post in June 1864. ∽ Six months later, on December 6, 1864, President Lincoln nominated Chase Chief Justice of the United States. The Senate confirmed the appointment the same day. Chase served as Chief Justice for eight years and died on May 7, 1873, at the age of sixty-five. ∽

MORRISON R. WAITE

Chief Justice 1874 – 1888

MORRISON R. WAITE was born in Lyme, Connecticut, on November 29, 1816. He was graduated from Yale College in 1837 and moved to Ohio to read law with an attorney in Maumee City. Waite was admitted to the bar in 1839 and practiced in Maumee City until 1850. He then moved to Toledo, where he practiced until 1874. ❧ Waite was elected to the Ohio General Assembly in 1850 and served one term. He ran unsuccessfully for the United States House of Representatives in 1846 and 1862. Waite declined an appointment to the Ohio Supreme Court in 1863. ❧ In 1871, President Ulysses S. Grant appointed Waite to a Commission established to settle United States claims against Great Britain, arising out of the latter's assistance to the Confederacy during the Civil War. The proceedings resulted in an award of $15.5 million in compensation to the United States. ❧ Upon his return from Europe, Waite was elected to the Ohio Constitutional Convention of 1873 and was unanimously selected to serve as its president. ❧ During the Convention, on January 19, 1874, President Grant nominated Waite Chief Justice of the United States. The Senate confirmed the appointment two days later. Waite served as Chief Justice for fourteen years and died on March 23, 1888, at the age of seventy-one. ❧

MELVILLE WESTON FULLER

Chief Justice 1888 – 1910

MELVILLE WESTON FULLER was born in Augusta, Maine, on February 11, 1833, and was graduated from Bowdoin College in 1853. Fuller read law in Bangor, Maine, and was admitted to the bar after six months of study at Harvard Law School. ∞ In 1855, Fuller began to practice law in Augusta, Maine, and was elected President of the Augusta Common Council and appointed city solicitor. ∞ In 1856, Fuller moved west to Chicago, where he established a law practice and became active in politics. He was elected to the Illinois House of Representatives in 1863 and served one term. In succeeding years he was offered the positions of Chairman of the Civil Service Commission and Solicitor General of the United States but declined both. ∞ President Grover Cleveland nominated Fuller Chief Justice of the United States on April 30, 1888. The Senate confirmed the appointment on July 20, 1888. ∞ While on the Court, Fuller served on the Venezuela-British Guiana Border Commission and the Court of Permanent Arbitration at the Hague. ∞ Fuller served twenty-one years as Chief Justice and died on July 4, 1910, at the age of seventy-seven. ∞

EDWARD DOUGLASS WHITE

Chief Justice 1910 – 1921 ∞ Associate Justice 1894 – 1910

EDWARD DOUGLASS WHITE was born in the Parish of Lafourche, Louisiana, on November 3, 1845. While White was studying at Georgetown College (now Georgetown University) the Civil War began and he returned home to join the Confederate Army. He was captured in 1863 by Union troops and remained in captivity until the end of the War. ∞ Upon his release in 1865, White read law and attended the University of Louisiana. He was admitted to the bar in 1866 and established a law practice in New Orleans. ∞ White was elected to the Louisiana State Senate in 1874, and from 1878 to 1880 he served on the Louisiana Supreme Court. In 1891, the State Legislature elected him to the United States Senate. ∞ President Grover Cleveland nominated White to the Supreme Court of the United States on February 19, 1894. The Senate confirmed the appointment the same day. ∞ White had served for sixteen years on the Court when, on December 12, 1910, President William H. Taft nominated him Chief Justice of the United States. The Senate confirmed the appointment the same day. White was the first Associate Justice to be appointed Chief Justice. ∞ White served on the Court for a total of twenty-six years, ten of them as Chief Justice. He died on May 19, 1921, at the age of seventy-five. ∞

WILLIAM HOWARD TAFT
Chief Justice 1921 – 1930

WILLIAM HOWARD TAFT was born in Cincinnati, Ohio, on September 15, 1857. He was graduated from Yale University in 1878 and from Cincinnati Law School in 1880. ∞ Taft began his career in private practice in Cincinnati. After serving as an assistant prosecutor and a Judge of the Ohio Superior Court, he was appointed Solicitor General of the United States in 1890. From 1892 to 1900, Taft served as a Judge on the United States Court of Appeals for the Sixth Circuit. In 1901, he was named Civilian Governor of the Philippines. In 1904, President Theodore Roosevelt appointed Taft Secretary of War. ∞ Taft was elected President of the United States in 1908 and served one term. After leaving the White House, Taft taught constitutional law at Yale University and appeared frequently on the lecture circuit. From 1918 to 1919, he served as Joint Chairman of the War Labor Board. ∞ President Warren G. Harding nominated Taft Chief Justice of the United States on June 30, 1921. The Senate confirmed the appointment the same day, making Taft the only person in history to have been both President and Chief Justice. As Chief Justice he focused on the administration of justice and at his request Congress created the Conference of Senior Circuit (Chief) Judges to oversee court administration. This body became the Judicial Conference of the United States. Taft retired from the Court on February 3, 1930, after serving eight years as Chief Justice. He died on March 8, 1930, at the age of seventy-two. ∞

CHARLES EVANS HUGHES

Chief Justice 1930 – 1941 ∞ *Associate Justice* 1910 – 1916

CHARLES EVANS HUGHES was born in Glens Falls, New York, on April 11, 1862. He was graduated in 1881 from Brown University and received a law degree from Columbia University in 1884. For the next twenty years, he practiced law in New York, New York, with only a three-year break to teach law at Cornell University. ∞ Hughes was elected Governor of New York in 1905 and re-elected two years later. On April 25, 1910, President William H. Taft nominated Hughes to the Supreme Court of the United States, and the Senate confirmed the appointment on May 2, 1910. ∞ Hughes resigned from the Court in 1916 upon being nominated by the Republican Party to run for President. After losing the election to Woodrow Wilson, he returned to his law practice in New York. ∞ Hughes served as Secretary of State from 1921 to 1925. He subsequently resumed his law practice while serving in the Hague as a United States delegate to the Permanent Court of Arbitration from 1926 to 1930 and on the Permanent Court of International Justice from 1928 to 1930. ∞ On February 3, 1930, President Herbert Hoover nominated Hughes Chief Justice of the United States, and the Senate confirmed the appointment on February 13, 1930. He served as Chairman of the Judicial Conference of the United States from 1930 to 1941. Hughes retired on July 1, 1941, after serving eleven years as Chief Justice. He died on August 27, 1948, at the age of eighty-six. ∞

HARLAN FISKE STONE

Chief Justice 1941 – 1946 ∞ *Associate Justice* 1925 – 1941

HARLAN FISKE STONE was born on October 11, 1872, in Chesterfield, New Hampshire. He was graduated from Amherst College in 1894. After teaching high school chemistry for one year, he studied law at Columbia University, where he received his degree in 1898. ∞ In 1899, Stone was admitted to the bar and joined a New York law firm. For the next twenty-five years he divided his time between his practice and a career as a professor of law at Columbia University. He became Dean of the Law School in 1910 and remained in that position for thirteen years. ∞ In 1924, President Calvin Coolidge appointed Stone Attorney General of the United States. The following year, on January 5, 1925, President Coolidge nominated him to the Supreme Court of the United States. The Senate confirmed the appointment February 5, 1925. After sixteen years of service as an Associate Justice, Stone was nominated Chief Justice of the United States by President Franklin D. Roosevelt on June 12, 1941. The Senate confirmed the appointment on June 27, 1941. He served as Chairman of the Judicial Conference of the United States from 1941 to 1946. ∞ Stone served a total of twenty years on the Court. He died on April 22, 1946, at the age of seventy-three. ∞

FRED M. VINSON

Chief Justice 1946 – 1953

FRED M. VINSON was born in Louisa, Kentucky, on January 22, 1890. He was graduated from Centre College in 1909 and from its Law School two years later. In 1911, Vinson was admitted to the bar and began to practice law in Ashland, Kentucky. ∞ Vinson became City Attorney of Ashland and, in 1921, Commonwealth's Attorney for the County. He was elected to the United States House of Representatives in 1924 and was re-elected in 1926. He resumed his Ashland practice for two years and then won re-election to the House for four consecutive terms. In 1938, President Franklin D. Roosevelt appointed him to the United States Court of Appeals for the District of Columbia Circuit. ∞ Vinson served the Roosevelt Administration during World War II in a succession of positions starting in 1943: Director of the Office of Economic Stabilization, Administrator of the Federal Loan Agency, and Director of the Office of War Mobilization and Reconversion. In 1945, shortly after the end of the War, President Harry Truman appointed Vinson Secretary of the Treasury. ∞ On June 6, 1946, President Truman nominated Vinson Chief Justice of the United States. The Senate confirmed the appointment on June 20, 1946. He served as Chairman of the Judicial Conference of the United States from 1946 to 1953. Vinson served for seven years as Chief Justice and died on September 8, 1953, at the age of sixty-three. ∞

EARL WARREN

Chief Justice 1953 – 1969

EARL WARREN was born in Los Angeles, California, on March 19, 1891. He was graduated from the University of California in 1912 and received a law degree in 1914. He practiced for a time in law offices in San Francisco and Oakland. ∞ In 1919, Warren became Deputy City Attorney of Oakland, beginning a life in public service. In 1920, he became Deputy Assistant District Attorney of Alameda County. In 1925, he was appointed District Attorney of Alameda County, to fill an unexpired term, and was elected and re-elected to the office in his own right in 1926, 1930, and 1934. In 1938, he was elected Attorney General of California. ∞ In 1942, Warren was elected Governor of California, and he was twice re-elected. In 1948, he was the Republican nominee for Vice President of the United States and, in 1952, he sought the Republican party's nomination for President. ∞ On September 30, 1953, President Dwight D. Eisenhower nominated Warren Chief Justice of the United States under a recess appointment. The Senate confirmed the appointment on March 1, 1954. Warren served as Chairman of the Judicial Conference of the United States from 1953 to 1969 and as Chairman of the Federal Judicial Center from 1968 to 1969. He also chaired the commission of inquiry into the assassination of President John F. Kennedy in 1963. He retired on June 23, 1969, after fifteen years of service, and died on July 9, 1974, at the age of eighty-three. ∞

WARREN E. BURGER

Chief Justice 1969 – 1986

WARREN E. BURGER was born in St. Paul, Minnesota, on September 17, 1907. After pre-legal studies at the University of Minnesota in night classes, he earned a law degree in 1931 from the St. Paul College of Law (now the William Mitchell College of Law) by attending four years of night classes while working in the accounting department of a life insurance company. ∞ He was appointed to the faculty of his law school upon graduation and remained on the adjunct faculty until 1946. Burger practiced with a St. Paul law firm from 1931 to 1953. In 1953, President Dwight D. Eisenhower appointed Burger Assistant Attorney General of the United States, Chief of the Civil Division of the Department of Justice. In 1955, President Eisenhower appointed him to the United States Court of Appeals for the District of Columbia Circuit, where he served until 1969. ∞ President Richard M. Nixon nominated Burger Chief Justice of the United States on May 22, 1969. The Senate confirmed the appointment on June 9, 1969, and he took office on June 23, 1969. ∞ In July 1985, President Ronald Reagan appointed Burger Chairman of the Commission on the Bicentennial of the United States Constitution. As Chief Justice he served as Chairman of the Judicial Conference of the United States and as Chairman of the Federal Judicial Center from 1969 to 1986. ∞ Burger retired from the Court on September 26, 1986, after seventeen years of service, and continued to direct the Commission on the Bicentennial of the United States Constitution from 1986 to 1992. ∞

WILLIAM H. REHNQUIST
Chief Justice 1986 – ∞ *Associate Justice* 1972 – 1986

WILLIAM H. REHNQUIST was born in Milwaukee, Wisconsin, on October 1, 1924. He served in World War II with the Army Air Corps. When the War ended, Rehnquist entered Stanford University and was graduated in 1948 with both an undergraduate and a master's degree. He earned a second master's degree from Harvard University in 1950 before enrolling in Stanford University Law School. After graduation from Stanford Law School in 1952, Rehnquist served as law clerk to Supreme Court Associate Justice Robert H. Jackson for the 1952-1953 Term. ∞ Rehnquist settled in Phoenix, Arizona, the following year and engaged in the practice of law for sixteen years until 1969, when President Richard M. Nixon appointed him Assistant Attorney General for the Office of Legal Counsel in the Department of Justice. On October 21, 1971, President Nixon nominated Rehnquist as an Associate Justice of the Supreme Court of the United States. The Senate confirmed the appointment on December 10, 1971. ∞ After serving for fifteen years as an Associate Justice, President Ronald Reagan nominated him Chief Justice of the United States on June 17, 1986. The Senate confirmed the appointment on September 17, 1986. As Chief Justice he serves as Chairman of the Judicial Conference of the United States and as Chairman of the Federal Judicial Center. ∞

I DO SOLEMNLY SWEAR

THAT I WILL ADMINISTER JUSTICE WITHOUT RESPECT TO PERSONS,

DO EQUAL RIGHT TO THE POOR AND TO THE RICH,

AND THAT I WILL IMPARTIALLY DISCHARGE AND PERFORM

ALL THE DUTIES INCUMBENT ON ME,

ACCORDING TO THE BEST OF MY ABILITIES AND UNDERSTANDING

AGREEABLY TO THE CONSTITUTION AND LAWS OF THE UNITED STATES

SO HELP ME GOD.

JUDICIAL OATH, JUDICIARY ACT, SECTION 8, 1789

Associate Justices

of the United States 1789 – 1991

JAMES WILSON
Associate Justice 1789 – 1798

AMES WILSON was born in Caskardy, Scotland, on September 14, 1742. He entered St. Andrews University in 1757 and emigrated to America in 1765 to take a teaching position at the College of Philadelphia. He read law with an attorney and in 1768 began a private law practice in Reading, Pennsylvania. ∞ Wilson was elected a delegate to the First Continental Congress in 1775 and was a signer of the Declaration of Independence. He also served as a delegate to the Second Continental Congress. ∞ As a delegate to the Constitutional Convention in Philadelphia in 1787, Wilson was a member of the committee that produced the first draft of the Constitution. He signed the finished document on September 17, 1787, and later served as a delegate to the Pennsylvania Ratification Convention. ∞ On September 24, 1789, President George Washington nominated Wilson one of the original Associate Justices of the Supreme Court of the United States. The Senate confirmed the appointment two days later. ∞ Wilson served on the Supreme Court for eight years and died on August 21, 1798, at the age of fifty-five. ∞

WILLIAM CUSHING

Associate Justice 1790 – 1810

WILLIAM CUSHING was born on March 1, 1732, in Scituate, Massachusetts. After graduation from Harvard College in 1751, Cushing taught school for one year in Roxbury, Massachusetts, and then read law in Boston. He was admitted to practice in 1755. ∞ In 1760, Cushing moved to Lincoln County, Massachusetts (now Dresden, Maine), to become a Probate Judge and Justice of the Peace. In 1772, he was appointed to the Superior Court of Massachusetts Bay Province. ∞ Under the new State Government, Cushing was retained as a Justice of the Massachusetts Superior Court, and in 1777 he was elevated to Chief Justice. From 1780 to 1789, he served as Chief Justice of the Massachusetts Supreme Judicial Court. Cushing strongly supported ratification of the United States Constitution and served as Vice Chairman of the Massachusetts Ratification Convention. ∞ On September 24, 1789, President George Washington nominated Cushing one of the original Associate Justices of the Supreme Court of the United States. The Senate confirmed the appointment two days later. ∞ Cushing served on the Supreme Court for twenty years and died on September 13, 1810, at the age of seventy-eight. ∞

JOHN BLAIR, JR.
Associate Justice 1790–1796

JOHN BLAIR, JR., was born in Williamsburg, Virginia, in 1732. He was graduated from the College of William and Mary in 1754. After one year of law study in England at the Middle Temple, London, he returned to Virginia to practice law. ∞ Blair began his public service in 1766 as a member of the Virginia House of Burgesses. In 1770, he resigned from the House to become Clerk of the Governor's Council. Blair was a delegate to the Virginia Convention of 1776, which drafted the State Constitution. ∞ Blair became a Judge of the Virginia General Court in 1777 and was elevated to Chief Judge in 1779. From 1780 to 1789, he served as a Judge of the First Virginia Court of Appeals. ∞ Blair was a delegate to the Federal Constitutional Convention of 1787 and was one of three Virginia delegates to sign the Constitution. He was also a delegate to the Virginia Ratification Convention of 1788. ∞ On September 24, 1789, President George Washington nominated Blair one of the original Associate Justices of the Supreme Court of the United States. The Senate confirmed the appointment two days later. ∞ Blair served five years on the Supreme Court. Citing the rigors of circuit riding and ill health, he resigned on January 27, 1796. Blair died on August 31, 1800, at the age of sixty-eight. ∞

JAMES IREDELL

Associate Justice 1790 – 1799

JAMES IREDELL was born on October 5, 1751, in Lewes, England. He was educated in England and in 1768 became Colonial Comptroller of Customs in Edenton, North Carolina. While serving in that position, Iredell read law and was admitted to practice in 1770. ∞ In 1776, he resigned from his position with Customs and joined the independence movement. When North Carolina severed its ties with the British Crown, Iredell served on a commission to redraft the state's laws. In 1778, the Superior Court of North Carolina was created and Iredell was named one of its three Judges. He resigned after a few months because of the rigors of circuit riding and resumed his law practice. He served as Attorney General of North Carolina from 1779 to 1781. ∞ Under a new state constitution, Iredell codified the laws of North Carolina. In 1788, he served as floor leader of the Federalists in the North Carolina Ratification Convention. ∞ On February 8, 1790, President George Washington nominated Iredell to the Supreme Court of the United States. The Senate confirmed the appointment two days later. Iredell served for nine years on the Supreme Court and died on October 20, 1799, at the age of forty-eight. ∞

THOMAS JOHNSON

Associate Justice 1792 – 1793

THOMAS JOHNSON was born on November 4, 1732, in Calvert County, Maryland. He was educated at home and studied law in the office of the Clerk of the Provincial Court in Annapolis, and later with an Annapolis attorney. He was admitted to the Maryland bar in 1760. ∞ Johnson began his public career in 1762 as a delegate to the Maryland Provincial Assembly. He served as a delegate to the First and Second Continental Congresses, and in 1776, he helped draft the Maryland constitution. During the Revolutionary War, Johnson served in the Maryland Militia. In 1777, he became the first Governor of the State of Maryland and served three consecutive terms. ∞ In 1788, Johnson served as a delegate to the Maryland Ratification Convention. On April 20, 1790, he was appointed Chief Judge of the General Court of Maryland, the highest common law court in the State. ∞ On November 1, 1791, President George Washington nominated Johnson to the Supreme Court of the United States. The Senate confirmed the appointment on November 7, 1791. ∞ Citing the rigors of circuit riding, Johnson resigned from the Supreme Court on February 1, 1793. He died on October 26, 1819, at the age of eighty-six. ∞

WILLIAM PATERSON
Associate Justice 1793 – 1806

WILLIAM PATERSON was born on December 24, 1745, in County Antrim, Ireland. His family emigrated to America two years later and eventually settled in Princeton, New Jersey. Paterson was graduated from the College of New Jersey (now Princeton University) in 1763 and earned a graduate degree in 1766. He read law, was admitted to the bar in 1769, and established a law practice. ∞ During the Revolutionary War, Paterson served as an officer with the Somerset County Minutemen and was a member of the Council of Safety. He was elected a delegate to the Provincial Congress of New Jersey in 1775 and to the State Constitutional Convention in 1776. After helping draft the New Jersey Constitution, he became Attorney General of that State, serving from 1776 to 1783. ∞ Paterson was a delegate to the Constitutional Convention of 1787 and, as a Senator in the First Federal Congress, he helped to draft the Judiciary Act of 1789, which established the federal court system. He left the Senate in 1790 to become Governor and Chancellor of New Jersey. ∞ President George Washington nominated Paterson to the Supreme Court of the United States on March 4, 1793, and the Senate confirmed the appointment the same day. Paterson served for thirteen years on the Supreme Court and died on September 9, 1806, at the age of sixty. ∞

SAMUEL CHASE

Associate Justice 1796 – 1811

SAMUEL CHASE was born in Somerset County, Maryland, on April 17, 1741. He read law in the office of an Annapolis attorney and was admitted to the bar in 1761. He practiced law at the Mayor's Court in Annapolis and appeared before other courts throughout the County. ∞ In 1764, Chase was elected to the Maryland General Assembly and served there for twenty years. He served as a delegate to the First and Second Continental Congresses and signed the Declaration of Independence. ∞ Following the Revolutionary War, he served as a Judge of the Baltimore Criminal Court from 1788 to 1796 and as Chief Judge of the General Court of Maryland from 1791 to 1796. ∞ President George Washington nominated Chase to the Supreme Court of the United States on January 26, 1796, and the Senate confirmed the appointment the following day. In 1803, Chase became the only Justice of the Supreme Court in history to be impeached, but the Senate refused to convict him and the bill of impeachment was dismissed. ∞ Chase served on the Supreme Court for fifteen years and died on June 19, 1811, at the age of seventy. ∞

BUSHROD WASHINGTON
Associate Justice 1799 – 1829

BUSHROD WASHINGTON was born on June 5, 1762, in Westmoreland County, Virginia. He was a nephew of the first President of the United States, George Washington. He was graduated from the College of William and Mary in 1778 and attended a course of law lectures conducted by George Wythe at the same time as did John Marshall, who later became Chief Justice of the United States. ∞ Washington enlisted in the Continental Army near the end of the Revolution and was present at the surrender of Cornwallis at Yorktown. After the War, he resumed his law studies in the Philadelphia office of James Wilson, who preceded him on the Supreme Court. ∞ Washington began a private law practice in Westmoreland County, Virginia, and then moved to Alexandria, Virginia. In 1787, he was elected to the Virginia House of Delegates, and in 1788 he served as a delegate to the Virginia Convention which ratified the Constitution. ∞ In 1790, Washington moved to Richmond, Virginia, where he continued his law practice. He served as a reporter for the Court of Appeals and also instructed many law students, including Henry Clay. President John Adams nominated Washington to the Supreme Court of the United States on December 19, 1798. The Senate confirmed the appointment the following day. Washington served on the Supreme Court for thirty years. He died on November 26, 1829, at the age of sixty-seven. ∞

ALFRED MOORE

Associate Justice 1800 – 1804

ALFRED MOORE was born on May 21, 1755, in New Hanover County, North Carolina. He was sent to school in Boston and read law under the guidance of his father, a colonial judge. Moore was admitted to the bar in 1775 at the age of twenty. ∞ During the Revolutionary War, Moore served as a captain in a Continental regiment. After his father's death in 1777, Moore returned home and joined the militia. In 1782, he was elected to the North Carolina State Legislature and, later that year, he was appointed Attorney General of North Carolina. In 1792, he was elected to the State Legislature for the second time. Three years later, Moore lost a bid for a seat in the United States Senate. In 1798, President John Adams appointed Moore to a commission to negotiate a treaty with the Cherokee Indians. He resigned the following year to become a Judge of the North Carolina Superior Court. ∞ On December 6, 1799, President John Adams nominated Moore to the Supreme Court of the United States. The Senate confirmed the appointment on December 10, 1799. Moore served three years on the Supreme Court. He resigned on January 26, 1804. He died on October 15, 1810, at the age of fifty-five. ∞

WILLIAM JOHNSON
Associate Justice 1804 – 1834

WILLIAM JOHNSON was born on December 17, 1771, in Charleston, South Carolina. During the Revolutionary War, his father was imprisoned by the British and the family was exiled to Philadelphia, Pennsylvania. ∞ Johnson was graduated from the College of New Jersey (now Princeton University) in 1790, and studied law in a Charleston law office. ∞ Johnson was admitted to the bar in 1793, and the following year he was elected to the South Carolina House of Representatives. He served three consecutive terms, the third term as Speaker. ∞ In 1799, the South Carolina Legislature elected Johnson to one of the three seats on the Court of Common Pleas, the highest court in the State. ∞ Johnson had served on the Court of Common Pleas for four years when, on March 22, 1804, President Thomas Jefferson nominated him to the Supreme Court of the United States. The Senate confirmed the appointment two days later. ∞ Johnson served on the Supreme Court for thirty years. He died on August 4, 1834, at the age of sixty-two. ∞

H. BROCKHOLST LIVINGSTON
Associate Justice 1807 – 1823

BROCKHOLST LIVINGSTON was born in New York, New York, on November 25, 1757. He was graduated from the College of New Jersey (now Princeton University) in 1774 and planned to study law. With the outbreak of the Revolutionary War, however, Livingston joined the Continental Army. ∾ Livingston participated in the siege of Ticonderoga, served as an aide to General Benedict Arnold in the Saratoga campaign, and witnessed General John Burgoyne's surrender in 1777. In 1779, he served on a diplomatic mission to Spain as private secretary to John Jay, who later became the first Chief Justice of the United States. ∾ As the War drew to a close, Livingston resumed the study of law in Albany, New York. He was admitted to the bar in 1783 and settled in New York, New York, where he practiced law. From 1784 until his death he served as a Trustee and Treasurer of Columbia University. ∾ In 1786, Livingston was elected to the New York Assembly and served for three years. He was appointed to the New York Supreme Court in 1802 and served for five years. ∾ President Thomas Jefferson nominated Livingston to the Supreme Court of the United States on December 13, 1806, and the Senate confirmed the appointment on December 17, 1806. He served on the Supreme Court for sixteen years. Livingston died on March 18, 1823, at the age of sixty-five. ∾

Thomas Todd

Associate Justice 1807 – 1826

THOMAS TODD was born in King and Queen County, Virginia, on January 23, 1765. He lost both of his parents at an early age and was raised by a guardian. At the age of sixteen, Todd served in the Revolutionary War for six months and then returned home to attend Liberty Hall (now Washington and Lee University). Upon graduation in 1783, Todd became a tutor at Liberty Hall in exchange for room and board and instruction in the law. ∞ In 1784, Todd moved to Danville, Kentucky, which was then still part of Virginia. Kentucky was seeking statehood, and Todd served as the clerk at five conventions held for that purpose. He was admitted to the bar in 1788 and entered the practice of law. Todd served as secretary to the State Legislature when Kentucky was admitted to the Union in 1792, and when the Kentucky Court of Appeals, the State's highest court, was created in 1789, he became its chief clerk. ∞ In 1801, Todd was appointed a Justice of the Kentucky Court of Appeals, and in 1806 he was elevated to Chief Justice. ∞ On February 28, 1807, President Thomas Jefferson nominated Todd to the Supreme Court of the United States. The Senate confirmed the appointment on March 3, 1807. Todd served on the Supreme Court for eighteen years. He died on February 7, 1826, at the age of sixty-one. ∞

GABRIEL DUVALL

Associate Justice 1811 – 1835

GABRIEL DUVALL was born on December 6, 1752, in Prince Georges County, Maryland. He studied classics and law and was admitted to the bar in 1778. ∽ During the Revolutionary War, Duvall served as mustermaster and commissary of stores for the Maryland troops and later as a private in the Maryland militia. He served as Clerk of the Maryland State Convention from 1775 to 1777, and after the Maryland State Government was created in 1777, he served as clerk for the House of Delegates. ∽ Duvall was elected to the Maryland State Council in 1782 and to the Maryland House of Delegates in 1787. He served until 1794, when he was elected to the United States House of Representatives. Duvall was re-elected but resigned on March 28, 1796, to become Chief Justice of the General Court of Maryland. ∽ President Thomas Jefferson appointed Duvall the first Comptroller of the Treasury on December 15, 1802, and he served nine years in that position. On November 15, 1811, President James Madison nominated Duvall to the Supreme Court of the United States. The Senate confirmed the appointment three days later. ∽ Duvall served on the Supreme Court for twenty-three years and resigned on January 14, 1835. He died on March 6, 1844, at the age of ninety-one. ∽

JOSEPH STORY

Associate Justice 1812 – 1845

JOSEPH STORY was born on September 18, 1779, in Marblehead, Massachusetts. He was graduated from Harvard College in 1798. Story read law in the offices of two Marblehead attorneys and was admitted to the bar in 1801. He established a law practice in Salem, Massachusetts. ∞ In 1805, Story served one term in the Massachusetts Legislature, and in 1808 he was elected to the United States House of Representatives. After one term, he returned to the Massachusetts Lower House, and in 1811 he was elected Speaker. On November 15, 1811, President James Madison nominated Story to the Supreme Court of the United States. The Senate confirmed the appointment on November 18, 1811. At the age of thirty-two, Story was the youngest person ever appointed to the Supreme Court. ∞ While on the Supreme Court, Story served as a delegate to the Massachusetts Constitutional Convention of 1820 and was a Professor of Law at Harvard, where he wrote a series of nine commentaries on the law, each of which was published in several editions. ∞ Story served on the Supreme Court for thirty-three years. He died on September 10, 1845, at the age of sixty-five. ∞

SMITH THOMPSON

Associate Justice 1823 – 1843

SMITH THOMPSON was born about January 17, 1768, in Dutchess County, New York. He was graduated from Princeton University in 1788 and taught school and read law with an attorney in Poughkeepsie. In 1793, he joined a Poughkeepsie law firm. ∽ In 1800, Thompson was elected to the New York State Legislature, and one year later he served as a delegate to the New York State Constitutional Convention. In 1802, Thompson was appointed State District Attorney for the Middle District of New York, but before assuming his duties he was appointed to the New York Supreme Court. He served there as an Associate Justice for twelve years and was named Chief Justice in 1814. ∽ Thompson resigned from the New York Supreme Court in 1818 to accept an appointment as Secretary of the Navy from President James Monroe. He served in the cabinet until 1823 when, on December 8, President Monroe nominated him to the Supreme Court of the United States. Thompson gave up plans to run for President in 1824 and accepted the Supreme Court appointment. The Senate confirmed the appointment on December 19, 1823. ∽ Thompson served on the Supreme Court for twenty years. In 1828, while still on the Court, he made an unsuccessful run for Governor of New York. Thompson died on December 18, 1843, at the age of seventy-five. ∽

ROBERT TRIMBLE

Associate Justice 1826 – 1828

ROBERT TRIMBLE was born in Augusta County, Virginia (now West Virginia), on November 17, 1776, and grew up in Kentucky. Trimble attended what is now Transylvania University and read law under two attorneys. He was admitted to the bar in 1803 and established a law practice in Paris, Kentucky. ∞ Trimble was elected to the Kentucky House of Representatives in 1802 and served one term. In 1807, he was appointed to the Kentucky Court of Appeals. He resigned the following year and returned to his law practice. ∞ Trimble served as United States District Attorney from 1813 to 1817 but declined several other public offices, including the Chief Justiceship of Kentucky in 1810. ∞ President James Madison appointed Trimble to the District Court of Kentucky in 1817, and he served eight years in that position. ∞ President John Quincy Adams nominated Trimble to the Supreme Court of the United States on April 11, 1826. The Senate confirmed the appointment on May 9, 1826. Trimble served on the Supreme Court for two years and died on August 25, 1828, at the age of fifty-one. ∞

John McLean
Associate Justice 1830 – 1861

JOHN McLEAN was born in Morris County, New Jersey, on March 11, 1785. His family soon moved to western Virginia, then to Kentucky, and settled in Warren County, Ohio, in 1797. McLean began his legal career in Cincinnati in 1804 by working in the office of the clerk of the Hamilton County Court of Common Pleas and reading law in the office of a Cincinnati attorney. He was admitted to the bar in 1807 and moved to Lebanon, Ohio, where he combined a law practice with publication of a weekly newspaper. Beginning in 1810, he devoted himself fully to his law practice. McLean was appointed an examiner in the Federal Land Office in Cincinnati in 1811. In 1812, he was elected to the United States House of Representatives. Re-elected two years later, he resigned in 1816 to take a seat on the Ohio Supreme Court. In 1822, President James Monroe appointed McLean Commissioner of the General Land Office in Washington, D.C., and one year later McLean was appointed Postmaster General. President Andrew Jackson nominated McLean to the Supreme Court of the United States on March 6, 1829. The Senate confirmed the appointment the following day. McLean served on the Supreme Court for nearly thirty-two years. He died on April 4, 1861, at the age of seventy-six.

HENRY BALDWIN

Associate Justice 1830 – 1844

Henry Baldwin was born in New Haven, Connecticut, on January 14, 1780. He attended Yale College and was graduated in 1797. ∞ He moved immediately to Philadelphia, where he read law in a law office and was soon admitted to the Pennsylvania bar. He moved to Pittsburgh, where he established a law practice with two partners. ∞ Baldwin also became joint owner of a newspaper and other business enterprises. He served on the City's Public Safety Council during the War of 1812. ∞ In 1816, Baldwin was elected to the United States House of Representatives. He served as Chairman of the House Committee on Domestic Manufactures and was twice re-elected but was forced to resign because of ill health in 1822. ∞ Baldwin recovered and resumed his law practice and business interests in 1824, along with his civic activities and his role as an unofficial political leader of Allegheny County. ∞ On January 4, 1830, President Andrew Jackson nominated Baldwin to the Supreme Court of the United States. The Senate confirmed the appointment two days later. Baldwin served on the Supreme Court for fourteen years. He died on April 21, 1844, at the age of sixty-four. ∞

James M. Wayne

Associate Justice 1835 – 1867

James M. Wayne was born in Savannah, Georgia, around 1790. He was graduated from the College of New Jersey (now Princeton University) in 1808 and read law under three different lawyers in Savannah, Georgia, and New Haven, Connecticut. Wayne was admitted to the bar in 1811 and entered a law partnership in Savannah. ∞ During the War of 1812, Wayne served with a volunteer Georgia militia unit. He was elected to the Georgia State Legislature in 1815 and became Mayor of Savannah in 1817. In 1820, Wayne was elected to the Savannah Court of Common Pleas, and he was appointed to the Superior Court of Georgia two years later. ∞ Wayne left the Court in 1828 and ran successfully for election to the United States House of Representatives. He was re-elected twice and became Chairman of the House Committee on Foreign Relations. ∞ President Andrew Jackson nominated Wayne to the Supreme Court of the United States on January 7, 1835, and the Senate confirmed the appointment two days later. ∞ Wayne served on the Supreme Court for thirty-two years. He died on July 5, 1867, at the age of seventy-seven. ∞

PHILIP P. BARBOUR

Associate Justice 1836 – 1841

PHILIP P. BARBOUR was born in Orange County, Virginia, on May 25, 1783. He attended local public schools and, at the age of seventeen, began reading law. He moved to Kentucky to practice but soon returned to Virginia where he attended one session of the College of William and Mary in 1801. He was admitted to the Virginia bar and established a law practice the following year. ∞ Barbour was elected to the Virginia House of Delegates in 1812. He was elected to the United States House of Representatives in 1814 and was re-elected to four additional terms. He served as Speaker of the House from 1821 to 1823. ∞ Barbour did not seek re-election to the House in 1824 but accepted an appointment as a Judge on the General Court for the Eastern District of Virginia. He was chosen President of the Virginia Constitutional Convention in 1829. ∞ Barbour was elected for the sixth time to Congress in 1827. At the end of the term in 1830, he accepted an appointment from President Andrew Jackson to the United States District Court in Virginia. ∞ Five years later, on February 28, 1835, President Jackson nominated Barbour to the Supreme Court of the United States. The Senate confirmed the appointment on March 15, 1836. He served on the Supreme Court for four years and died on February 25, 1841, at the age of fifty-seven. ∞

JOHN CATRON

Associate Justice 1837 – 1865

JOHN CATRON was born of German ancestry in Pennsylvania in approximately 1786, but little is known about his early years. They appear to have been spent in Virginia and Kentucky. There is no record of his schooling. ⌗ In 1812, Catron moved to the Cumberland Mountains of Tennessee and served under General Andrew Jackson in the War of 1812. He was admitted to the Tennessee bar in 1815, and in 1818 he moved to Nashville, Tennessee, where he established a practice specializing in land law. ⌗ In 1824, he was elected to the Supreme Court of Errors and Appeals. In 1831, the Legislature created the office of Chief Justice of the Court and Catron was elected to the position. Under a further reorganization in 1834, the position of Chief Justice was abolished. Catron returned to private practice and became active in national politics. ⌗ When Congress expanded the Supreme Court of the United States from seven to nine members, President Andrew Jackson nominated Catron to one of the new seats on March 3, 1837. The Senate confirmed the appointment on March 8, 1837. ⌗ Catron served on the Supreme Court for twenty-eight years. He died on May 30, 1865, at the age of seventy-nine. ⌗

John McKinley

Associate Justice 1838 – 1852

John McKinley was born in Culpeper County, Virginia, on May 1, 1780, but at an early age moved with his family to Kentucky. He studied law on his own and was admitted to the bar in 1800. McKinley practiced law for a time in Frankfort, the state capital, and Louisville, the commercial center. McKinley then moved to Alabama and settled in Huntsville, where he became active in politics. ∽ McKinley was elected to the Alabama State Legislature in 1820, 1831, and 1836. In 1826, the Legislature elected him to the United States Senate, where he served until 1831. He was elected to the United States House of Representatives in 1833 and served one term. ∽ In 1837, Congress expanded the Supreme Court from seven to nine members. In that same year, the Alabama Legislature re-elected McKinley to the United States Senate. However, McKinley accepted an appointment to one of the two new Supreme Court seats from President Martin Van Buren on September 18, 1837. The Senate confirmed the appointment on September 25, 1837. ∽ McKinley served on the Supreme Court for fourteen years. He died on July 19, 1852, at the age of seventy-two. ∽

PETER V. DANIEL

Associate Justice 1842 – 1860

PETER V. DANIEL was born in Stafford County, Virginia, on April 24, 1784. He was educated by tutors and attended the College of New Jersey (now Princeton University) for one year, from 1802 to 1803. Daniel then returned to Virginia and read law in Richmond under Edmund Randolph, who had been Secretary of State and Attorney General under President George Washington. ∽ Daniel was admitted to the bar in 1808 and established a law practice. The following year, he was elected to the Virginia State Legislature. In 1812, he became a member of the Virginia Privy Council, an executive advisory and review body. In 1818, he was elected Lieutenant Governor of Virginia, retaining his Council seat. He occupied both of these positions for the next seventeen years. ∽ President Andrew Jackson appointed Daniel to the United States District Court for Eastern Virginia in 1836. ∽ President Martin Van Buren nominated Daniel to the Supreme Court of the United States on February 26, 1841. The Senate confirmed the appointment on March 2, 1841. ∽ Daniel served on the Supreme Court for eighteen years. He died on May 31, 1860, at the age of seventy-six. ∽

SAMUEL NELSON

Associate Justice 1845 – 1872

SAMUEL NELSON was born in Hebron, New York, on November 10, 1792. He was graduated from Middlebury College in 1813 and read law in a law firm in Salem, New York. Nelson was admitted to the bar in 1817 and established a practice in Cortland, New York. ∞ Nelson served as Postmaster of Cortland from 1820 to 1823 and as a delegate to the New York State Constitutional Convention in 1821. In 1823, Nelson was appointed to the Sixth Circuit of New York. He served on the New York Supreme Court from 1831 to 1845, eight years as Chief Justice of that Court. ∞ President John Tyler nominated Nelson to the Supreme Court of the United States on February 4, 1845. The Senate confirmed the appointment ten days later. In 1871, President Ulysses S. Grant appointed Nelson to a Commission established to settle United States claims against Great Britain, arising out of the latter's assistance to the Confederacy during the Civil War. The proceedings resulted in an award of $15.5 million in compensation to the United States. ∞ On November 28, 1872, Nelson retired from the Supreme Court after twenty-seven years of service. He died on December 13, 1873, at the age of eighty-one. ∞

LEVI WOODBURY

Associate Justice 1845 – 1851

LEVI WOODBURY was born on December 22, 1789, in Francestown, New Hampshire. He was graduated from Dartmouth College in 1809, read law, and attended Tapping Reeve Law School. He was admitted to the bar in 1812 and practiced law in Francestown and nearby Portsmouth, New Hampshire. ∞ In 1816, Woodbury was appointed Clerk of the State Senate, and after one year he was placed on the New Hampshire Superior Court, where he served until 1823, when he was elected Governor of New Hampshire. ∞ In 1825, Woodbury was elected to the New Hampshire House of Representatives and became Speaker. Later the same year the State Legislature elected him to the United States Senate, where he served until 1831. ∞ President Andrew Jackson appointed Woodbury Secretary of the Navy in 1831. Three years later, the President appointed him Secretary of the Treasury, in which he served until 1841 when he was again elected to the United States Senate. ∞ President James K. Polk nominated Woodbury to the Supreme Court of the United States on December 23, 1845. The Senate confirmed the appointment on January 3, 1846, making him the first Associate Justice to have attended a law school. Woodbury served on the Supreme Court for five years and died on September 4, 1851, at the age of sixty-one. ∞

ROBERT C. GRIER
Associate Justice 1846 – 1870

ROBERT C. GRIER was born March 5, 1794, in Cumberland County, Pennsylvania. He was tutored by his father until age seventeen, when he enrolled in Dickinson College. Grier was graduated in 1812 at the age of eighteen and remained at Dickinson College for one year as an instructor. ∞ Grier continued his teaching career at a small school headed by his father in Northumberland, Pennsylvania, where he taught subjects ranging from mathematics to Greek and in 1815 succeeded his father as principal of Northumberland Academy. While teaching, Grier read law and passed the bar in 1817. He began a practice immediately in Bloomsburg, Pennsylvania, and later practiced law for fifteen years in Danville, Pennsylvania. ∞ On May 4, 1833, Grier was appointed to the newly created State District Court of Allegheny County and served there for thirteen years. ∞ On August 3, 1846, President James K. Polk nominated Grier to the Supreme Court of the United States, and the Senate confirmed the appointment on August 4, 1846. ∞ Grier served twenty-three years on the Supreme Court. He discontinued circuit riding in 1862 and retired on January 31, 1870. He died less than one year later, on September 25, 1870, at the age of seventy-six. ∞

Benjamin R. Curtis

Associate Justice 1851 – 1857

Benjamin R. Curtis was born on November 4, 1809, in Watertown, Massachusetts. He attended Harvard College, graduating in 1829, and entered Harvard Law School. Curtis established a law practice in Northfield, Massachusetts, in 1831 and received his law degree in 1832. ∞ In 1834, he moved to Boston and joined a law firm. He was elected to the Massachusetts State Legislature in 1849, where he was appointed chairman of a committee charged with the reform of state judicial procedures. Two years later, Curtis presented the Massachusetts Practice Act of 1851. It was considered a model of judicial reform and was approved by the legislature without amendment. ∞ President Millard Fillmore nominated Curtis to the Supreme Court of the United States on December 11, 1851, and the Senate confirmed the appointment on December 29, 1851. ∞ Curtis resigned from the Supreme Court on September 30, 1857, after almost six years of service, and returned to his law practice in Boston. During the following fifteen years, he argued cases before the Supreme Court on a number of occasions. He died on September 15, 1874, at the age of sixty-four. ∞

JOHN A. CAMPBELL
Associate Justice 1853 – 1861

OHN A. CAMPBELL was born near Washington, Georgia, on June 24, 1811. He was graduated from the University of Georgia in 1825 at the age of fourteen. He attended West Point Military Academy for three years but withdrew following the death of his father. ∞ After reading law for one year, Campbell was admitted to the Georgia bar. He moved to Alabama and established a law practice in Montgomery. In 1837 he moved to Mobile and was elected to the Alabama State Legislature. He was re-elected in 1843. President Franklin Pierce nominated Campbell to the Supreme Court of the United States on March 21, 1853, and the Senate confirmed the appointment four days later. ∞ When the South seceded from the Union, Campbell represented the southern states in an unsuccessful effort to mediate the impending conflict with the Lincoln Administration. Campbell resigned from the Court on April 30, 1861. From 1862 to 1865, he served in the Confederacy as Assistant Secretary of War for conscription. ∞ When the War ended, Campbell was imprisoned by the Union Army for several months. He was released by order of President Andrew Johnson and moved to New Orleans, where he re-established a law practice. Campbell returned to the Supreme Court on several occasions to argue cases and died on March 12, 1889, at the age of seventy-seven. ∞

NATHAN CLIFFORD

Associate Justice 1858 – 1881

NATHAN CLIFFORD was born on August 18, 1803, in Rumney, New Hampshire. After reading law in the office of a local attorney, he was admitted to the bar in 1827 and moved to Newfield, Maine, to establish a law practice. ∞ Clifford was elected to the lower house of the Maine legislature in 1830 for a one-year term and was re-elected three times, serving as its Speaker during the last two terms. He was then elected Attorney General of Maine by the State Legislature and served in that position from 1834 to 1838. ∞ In 1838, Clifford was elected to the United States House of Representatives, where he served two terms. Defeated in a bid for a third term, he returned to his law practice in 1843. ∞ President James K. Polk appointed Clifford Attorney General of the United States in 1846. Two years later, President Polk appointed Clifford United States Minister to Mexico. ∞ Clifford returned to Maine in 1849 and resumed his law practice in the City of Portland. Six years later, on December 9, 1857, President James Buchanan nominated Clifford to the Supreme Court of the United States. The Senate confirmed the appointment on January 12, 1858. ∞ Clifford served on the Supreme Court for twenty-three years. He died on July 25, 1881, at the age of seventy-seven. ∞

Noah H. Swayne

Associate Justice 1862 – 1881

Noah h. swayne was born in Frederick County, Virginia, on December 7, 1804. At an early age he studied medicine under a physician in Alexandria, Virginia, but he eventually abandoned medicine to read law with an attorney in Warrenton, Virginia. He was admitted to the bar in 1823. ∞ Because of his opposition to slavery, in 1824 Swayne moved to the free state of Ohio. The following year he established a practice in Coshocton and was soon elected Prosecuting Attorney of Coshocton County. In 1829, he was elected to the State Legislature. ∞ In 1830, President Andrew Jackson appointed Swayne United States Attorney for Ohio. He moved to Columbus to discharge his new duties and retained the position under President Martin Van Buren until 1841. Swayne was elected to the Columbus City Council in 1834, and in 1836 served another term in the State Legislature as a representative of Franklin County. ∞ On January 21, 1862, President Abraham Lincoln nominated Swayne to the Supreme Court of the United States. The Senate confirmed the appointment on January 24, 1862. Swayne retired from the Supreme Court on January 25, 1881 after serving for eighteen years. He died on June 8, 1884, at the age of seventy-nine. ∞

SAMUEL F. MILLER

Associate Justice 1862 – 1890

AMUEL F. MILLER was born in Richmond, Kentucky, on April 5, 1816. He studied medicine at Transylvania University and received a degree in 1838. He became a physician and practiced for twelve years in Knox County. ∞ Miller developed an interest in legal and political matters and became a Justice of the Peace and member of the Knox County Court, an administrative body, in the 1840s. Miller shared an office with an attorney and began reading law. He was admitted to the bar in 1847 and established a law practice. ∞ Miller was opposed to slavery. When the Kentucky Constitutional Convention of 1849 proved inflexible on the question of eventual modification and abolition of slavery, Miller chose to move to a free state. He freed his slaves and settled in Keokuk, Iowa, where he joined a law firm and specialized in land-title, steamboat, and commercial law. Miller also became active politically and campaigned unsuccessfully for nomination as Governor in 1861. ∞ On July 16, 1862, President Abraham Lincoln nominated Miller to the Supreme Court of the United States as the first Justice from west of the Mississippi River. The Senate confirmed the appointment the same day. Miller served on the Supreme Court for twenty-eight years. He died on October 13, 1890, at the age of seventy-four. ∞

DAVID DAVIS

Associate Justice 1862 – 1877

AVID DAVIS was born in Cecil County, Maryland, on March 9, 1815. After graduation from Kenyon College in 1832, he moved to Massachusetts where he read law with a local judge. He then enrolled in Yale Law School and was graduated in 1835. ∞ Davis moved to Pekin, Illinois, to establish a practice, and one year later moved to Bloomington. He was elected to the State Legislature in 1845 and to the Illinois Constitutional Convention in 1847. ∞ In the Convention, Davis championed a popularly elected state judiciary to replace the existing system of election by the legislature. His views prevailed, and in 1848 he was elected a Circuit Court Judge. Re-elected twice, he served until 1862. Abraham Lincoln and Stephen Douglas were among the lawyers who tried cases in his court. ∞ On December 1, 1862, President Lincoln nominated Davis to the Supreme Court of the United States. The Senate confirmed the appointment one week later. ∞ Davis had served fourteen years on the Court when he was elected to the United States Senate by the Illinois State Legislature. He resigned from the Supreme Court and served one term in the Senate, retiring in 1883. Davis died three years later, on June 26, 1886, at the age of seventy-one. ∞

STEPHEN J. FIELD
Associate Justice 1863 – 1897

STEPHEN J. FIELD was born on November 4, 1816, in Haddam, Connecticut. He was graduated in 1837 from Williams College, and for the next four years read law with his brother's law firm. He was admitted to the bar in 1841 and practiced law with his brother for seven years. ∞ In 1849, after a trip to Europe, Field settled in Marysville, California. In 1850, he became the chief local administrative officer of Marysville. When California was admitted to the Union that same year, Field was elected to the State Legislature. There he drafted the criminal and civil codes for the new State. ∞ After he was defeated in a bid for the State Senate in 1851, Field resumed the private practice of law. In 1857, he was elected to the California Supreme Court, where he served for six years. ∞ On March 6, 1863, President Abraham Lincoln nominated Field to a newly created seat on the Supreme Court of the United States. The Senate confirmed the appointment four days later. ∞ Field retired from the Supreme Court on December 1, 1897, after thirty-four years of service. He died on April 9, 1899, at the age of eighty-two. ∞

WILLIAM STRONG

Associate Justice 1870 – 1880

WILLIAM STRONG was born in Somers, Connecticut, on May 6, 1808. He was graduated from Yale College in 1828 and taught school in Connecticut and New Jersey for four years. Strong also obtained a graduate degree from Yale in 1831 and attended its Law School briefly in 1832. He moved to Reading, Pennsylvania, where he was admitted to the bar in 1832 and established a law practice. ∞ Strong was elected to the Reading City Council. In 1846, he was elected to the United States House of Representatives; he was re-elected two years later. In 1857, Strong was elected to a fifteen-year term on the Pennsylvania Supreme Court, where he served for eleven years. He resigned in 1868 to resume his law practice. ∞ On February 7, 1870, President Ulysses S. Grant nominated Strong to the Supreme Court of the United States. The Senate confirmed the appointment on February 18, 1870. While on the Court, he was appointed a member of the electoral commission which decided the disputed Presidential election of 1876 in favor of Rutherford B. Hayes. ∞ Strong served on the Supreme Court for ten years. He retired on December 14, 1880, and died on August 19, 1895, at the age of eighty-seven. ∞

JOSEPH P. BRADLEY
Associate Justice 1870 – 1892

JOSEPH P. BRADLEY was born in Berne, New York, on March 14, 1813. He attended a country school and began teaching at the age of sixteen. He attended Rutgers University several years later and was graduated in 1836. ∞ Bradley studied law in the Office of the Collector of the Port of Newark, New Jersey, and was admitted to the bar in 1839. For thirty years, he specialized in the practice of patent, commercial, and railroad law. ∞ In 1862, after lobbying in Washington for a compromise settlement of the Civil War, Bradley was a Unionist candidate for the United States House of Representatives but did not win election. ∞ President Ulysses S. Grant nominated Bradley to the Supreme Court of the United States on February 7, 1870. The Senate confirmed the appointment on March 21, 1870. ∞ In 1877, Bradley served on the electoral commission created to decide the outcome of the disputed 1876 presidential election. The commission was divided seven to seven on partisan lines. Bradley voted with the Republicans on all issues, making Rutherford B. Hayes President by a margin of one electoral vote. ∞ Bradley served on the Supreme Court for twenty-one years. He died on January 22, 1892, at the age of seventy-eight. ∞

WARD HUNT

Associate Justice 1873 – 1882

W ARD HUNT was born in Utica, New York, on June 14, 1810. He was graduated from Union College in 1828 and studied law at a private academy in Litchfield, Connecticut. He continued his law studies as a clerk in the office of a Utica judge. ∞ Hunt was admitted to the bar in 1831 and established a law partnership in Utica, where he practiced for thirty-one years. In 1839, Hunt served one term in the New York Assembly, and in 1844 he was elected Mayor of Utica. ∞ In 1853, Hunt ran for a seat on the New York Supreme Court but lost the election. He was elected a judge of the New York Court of Appeals in 1865, the State's highest court, and in 1868 he became Chief Judge. The following year, the New York court system was reorganized, and Hunt became a Commissioner of Appeals, a position he held for three years. ∞ President Ulysses S. Grant nominated Hunt to the Supreme Court of the United States on December 3, 1872. The Senate confirmed the appointment on December 11, 1872. ∞ Hunt served on the Supreme Court for nine years and retired from the Court in 1882. He died on March 24, 1886, at the age of seventy-five. ∞

JOHN MARSHALL HARLAN
Associate Justice 1877 – 1911

JOHN MARSHALL HARLAN was born in Boyle County, Kentucky, on June 1, 1833. He was graduated from Centre College in 1850 at the age of seventeen. Harlan studied law at Transylvania University for two years and read law in his father's law office. In 1853, he was admitted to the bar and began to practice law. ∞ In 1858, Harlan served for one year as Franklin County Judge. He ran for the United States House of Representatives in 1859 but was narrowly defeated. During the Civil War, Harlan joined the Union Army and served as an officer. ∞ In 1863, Harlan resigned his commission and was elected Attorney General of Kentucky, serving for four years. He was the Republican candidate for Governor of Kentucky in 1875. ∞ President Rutherford B. Hayes nominated Harlan to the Supreme Court of the United States on October 17, 1877. The Senate confirmed the appointment on November 29, 1877. ∞ While on the Court, Harlan was appointed by President Benjamin Harrison in 1892 to represent the United States in the arbitration with Great Britain over fishing rights in the Bering Sea. Harlan served on the Supreme Court for thirty-four years, a tenure exceeded by only four other Justices. He died on October 14, 1911, at the age of seventy-eight. ∞

WILLIAM B. WOODS

Associate Justice 1881 – 1887

WILLIAM B. WOODS was born on August 3, 1824, in Newark, Ohio. He attended Western Reserve College for three years and then transferred to Yale College, where he received an undergraduate degree in 1845. ∞ Woods returned to Newark and read law with a local attorney. He was admitted to the bar in 1847, and he established a law practice with his former mentor. In 1856, he was elected Mayor of Newark. Two years later he was elected to the Ohio State House of Representatives and became Speaker. ∞ Woods joined the Union Army in 1862. He served at Shiloh and Vicksburg and with General William Sherman. He was mustered out of service in 1866 with the rank of Major General. He remained in the South and established a law practice in Bentonville, Alabama. Woods was elected Chancellor of the Middle Chancery Division of Alabama in 1868. President Ulysses S. Grant appointed Woods to the Circuit Court for the Fifth Circuit in 1869. ∞ President Rutherford B. Hayes nominated Woods to the Supreme Court of the United States on December 15, 1880. The Senate confirmed the appointment on December 21, 1880, making him the first Associate Justice appointed from a Confederate state after the Civil War. He served six years on the Supreme Court and died on May 14, 1887, at the age of sixty-two. ∞

STANLEY MATTHEWS
Associate Justice 1881 – 1889

STANLEY MATTHEWS was born in Cincinnati, Ohio, on July 21, 1824. After graduation from Kenyon College in 1840, he read law in Cincinnati. He moved to Maury County, Tennessee, and was admitted to the bar at the age of eighteen. ∞ Two years later, Matthews returned to Cincinnati, where he was appointed Assistant Prosecuting Attorney for Hamilton County. From 1851 to 1853, he served as a Judge of the Hamilton County Court of Common Pleas. Matthews was elected to the Ohio Senate in 1855, and in 1858 he was appointed United States Attorney for Southern Ohio. ∞ Matthews served as a volunteer in the Union Army during the Civil War but resigned his commission in 1863 when he was elected a Judge of the Superior Court of Cincinnati. Two years later, he returned to private practice. In 1877, he served as Counsel to the Hayes-Tilden Electoral Commission, and later that year, he was appointed United States Senator from Ohio to fill a vacancy. ∞ President Rutherford B. Hayes nominated Matthews to the Supreme Court of the United States on January 26, 1881, but the Senate took no action on his confirmation. Renominated by President James A. Garfield on March 14, 1881, Matthews was confirmed by the Senate on May 12, 1881. Matthews died on March 22, 1889, at the age of sixty-four. ∞

HORACE GRAY
Associate Justice 1882 – 1902

ORACE GRAY was born in Boston, Massachusetts, on March 24, 1828. He enrolled in Harvard College at the age of thirteen and was graduated four years later. After traveling abroad, he received his law degree at Harvard in 1849. ∞ Gray was admitted to the bar in 1851 and practiced law for the next thirteen years. In 1854, he began his judicial career as a reporter for the State Supreme Court. During his tenure, Gray edited sixteen volumes of court records which, with some independent legal writing, earned him a reputation for historical scholarship and legal research. ∞ While working as a court reporter, Gray also served as a counselor to the Governor of Massachusetts on legal and constitutional questions and, in particular, issues arising from the Civil War. ∞ Gray was appointed to the State Supreme Court as an Associate Justice in 1864, the youngest appointee in the history of the Court. He was elevated to Chief Justice nine years later. ∞ President Chester A. Arthur nominated Gray to the Supreme Court of the United States on December 19, 1881, and the Senate confirmed the appointment the following day. ∞ Gray served on the Supreme Court for twenty years. He submitted his resignation on July 9, 1902, to become effective on the appointment of his successor. Gray died on September 15, 1902, at the age of seventy-four. ∞

SAMUEL BLATCHFORD

Associate Justice 1882 – 1893

SAMUEL BLATCHFORD was born on March 9, 1820, in New York, New York. At the age of thirteen, he enrolled in Columbia College and was graduated four years later. ∞ While serving as private secretary to the Governor of New York from 1837 to 1841, Blatchford studied law. After being admitted to the bar in 1842, he practiced with his father's New York law firm for three years, and then joined a law firm in Auburn, New York. ∞ Blatchford compiled a twenty-four volume set of previously uncollected decisions of the United States Court of Appeals for the Second Circuit. Although he was of-fered a judgeship on New York's highest court, he chose to continue his law practice. ∞ Blatchford accepted his first judicial appointment on May 3, 1867, to the Federal District Court for the Southern District of New York. Five years later he was elevated to the United States Court of Appeals for the Second Circuit. ∞ On March 13, 1882, President Chester A. Arthur nominated Blatchford to the Supreme Court of the United States. The Senate confirmed the appointment two weeks later. ∞ Blatchford served on the Supreme Court for eleven years. He died on July 7, 1893, at the age of seventy-three. ∞

LUCIUS Q. C. LAMAR

Associate Justice 1888 – 1893

LUCIUS Q. C. LAMAR was born in Eatonton, Georgia, on September 17, 1825. He was graduated from Emory College in 1845 and read law in Macon, Georgia. After his admission to the bar in 1847, he moved to Oxford, Mississippi, to practice law. In 1852, Lamar returned to Georgia, established a law practice in Covington, and the next year won election to the Georgia Legislature. He returned to Mississippi in 1855, and in 1857 he was elected to the United States House of Representatives. ∞ Lamar resigned from Congress on the eve of the Civil War and served for two years as an officer in the Confederate Army. For the last two years of the War, Lamar served as a Judge Advocate for the Army of Northern Virginia under General Robert E. Lee. ∞ At the end of the War, Lamar returned to Mississippi to practice law. He received a pardon for his services to the Confederacy, and in 1872 he was re-elected to the United States House of Representatives. In 1877, he was elected to the United States Senate. Lamar resigned from the Senate during his second term to accept an appointment as Secretary of the Interior. ∞ President Cleveland nominated Lamar to the Supreme Court of the United States on December 6, 1887. The Senate confirmed the appointment on January 16, 1888. Lamar served five years on the Supreme Court and died on January 23, 1893, at the age of sixty-seven. ∞

DAVID J. BREWER

Associate Justice 1890 – 1910

AVID J. BREWER was born in Smyrna, Asia Minor, in what is now Izmir, Turkey, on June 20, 1837. His missionary family returned to the United States one year after Brewer's birth and settled in Wethersfield, Connecticut. ∞ Brewer attended Wesleyan University for two years and then transferred to Yale, where he was graduated in 1856. After reading law for one year, Brewer attended Albany Law School and was graduated in 1858. He then moved to Kansas, where he was admitted to the bar and established a law practice. ∞ In 1861, Brewer was appointed Commissioner of the Circuit Court in Leavenworth. Two years later, he was elected a Judge of the Probate and Criminal Courts of Leavenworth County. From 1865 to 1869, he served on the United States District Court for Kansas. Brewer was elected to the Kansas Supreme Court in 1870 and served for fourteen years. In 1884, President Chester A. Arthur appointed Brewer to the Circuit Court for the Eighth Circuit. ∞ Five years later, on December 4, 1889, President Benjamin Harrison nominated Brewer to the Supreme Court of the United States. The Senate confirmed the appointment on December 18, 1889. Brewer served on the Supreme Court for twenty years. He died on March 28, 1910, at the age of seventy-two. ∞

HENRY B. BROWN

Associate Justice 1891 – 1906

HENRY B. BROWN was born in South Lee, Massachusetts, on March 2, 1836. After graduation from Yale College in 1856, he studied abroad for one year. Upon his return to New England, Brown began reading law in Ellington, Connecticut, and then pursued further studies at the law schools of Yale and Harvard. ∞ In 1859, at the age of twenty-three, Brown moved to Detroit, Michigan, and was admitted to the bar. He then established a law practice and developed a specialty in maritime law. In the first year of his practice, Brown was appointed a Deputy United States Marshal for Detroit. Three years later, he was appointed an Assistant United States Attorney for the Eastern District of Michigan. Brown also held an interim appointment as Circuit Judge for Wayne County in 1868. ∞ In 1875, President Ulysses S. Grant appointed Brown to the United States District Court for Eastern Michigan, where he served for fourteen years. ∞ President Benjamin Harrison nominated Brown to the Supreme Court of the United States on December 23, 1890, and the Senate confirmed the appointment six days later. Brown retired from the Supreme Court on May 28, 1906, and died on September 4, 1913, at the age of seventy-seven. ∞

GEORGE SHIRAS, JR.

Associate Justice 1892 – 1903

EORGE SHIRAS, JR., was born in Pittsburgh, Pennsylvania, on January 26, 1832. He began his college education at Ohio University, and after two years transferred to Yale, where he received his undergraduate degree in 1853. Shiras enrolled in Yale Law School but soon left New Haven to read law in Pittsburgh. ∞ Shiras was admitted to the bar in 1855 and entered practice with his brother in Dubuque, Iowa. He returned to Pittsburgh three years later and joined the law firm, where he specialized in railroad and corporate law. ∞ Shiras practiced law for thirty-seven years. In 1881, he refused an offer of election to the United States Senate from the Pennsylvania State Legislature. He served as a Presidential elector in 1888. ∞ President Benjamin Harrison nominated Shiras to the Supreme Court of the United States on July 19, 1892. The Senate confirmed the appointment on July 26, 1892. ∞ Upon receiving the nomination, Shiras declared his intention to retire after ten years on the Supreme Court, and he did so on February 23, 1903. He died on August 2, 1924, at the age of ninety-two. ∞

HOWELL E. JACKSON

Associate Justice 1893 – 1895

HOWELL E. JACKSON was born on April 8, 1832, in Paris, Tennessee. He was graduated from West Tennessee College in 1849, and studied law at the University of Virginia from 1851 to 1852 and at Cumberland College in 1856. He was admitted to the bar and began practicing law in his hometown of Paris. In 1859, he moved to Memphis and established a law practice. ∞ Although opposed to secession, Jackson served the Confederacy during the Civil War as the receiver of stolen property. In 1875, he was appointed to the Court of Arbitration for Western Tennessee, a provisional court established to liquidate the backlog of cases created by the War. ∞ In 1880, Jackson was elected to the Tennessee House of Representatives and in 1881 to the United States Senate. He resigned his Senate seat before the end of his term to accept an appointment as a Federal Judge on the Sixth Circuit in 1886. In 1891, he became a judge of the newly established United States Court of Appeals for the Sixth Circuit. ∞ On February 2, 1893, President Benjamin Harrison nominated Jackson to the Supreme Court of the United States. The Senate confirmed the appointment on February 18, 1893. ∞ Jackson contracted tuberculosis in 1894 but he continued to serve on the Supreme Court until his death on August 8, 1895, at the age of sixty-three. ∞

RUFUS W. PECKHAM

Associate Justice 1896 – 1909

RUFUS W. PECKHAM was born on November 8, 1838, in Albany, New York. He was educated at the Albany Boys' Academy and studied privately in Philadelphia, Pennsylvania. After one year in Europe, Peckham returned to Albany and read law in his father's office and was admitted to the bar in 1859. ∞ Peckham was elected Albany County Attorney in 1869. In 1881, he was named Corporation Counsel to the City of Albany and served two years. In this position, he successfully prosecuted a number of criminal cases in railroad-express car robberies. In 1882, he ran unsuccessfully for a seat on the New York Court of Appeals, the State's highest tribunal. In 1883, he was elected to the New York Supreme Court, and three years later he was elected to the Court of Appeals. ∞ During these years, Peckham was politically active. He was instrumental in preventing the New York City Democratic organization from gaining control of the State Democratic Party. ∞ Peckham had served on the New York Court of Appeals for nine years when, on December 3, 1895, President Grover Cleveland nominated him to the Supreme Court of the United States. The Senate confirmed the appointment on December 9, 1895. Peckham served on the Supreme Court for thirteen years and died on October 24, 1909, at the age of seventy. ∞

JOSEPH MCKENNA
Associate Justice 1898 – 1925

JOSEPH MCKENNA was born on August 10, 1843, in Philadelphia, Pennsylvania. In the mid-1850s, the McKenna family moved to northern California, where McKenna studied law at the Benicia Collegiate Institute. He was graduated in 1865 and admitted to the California bar in 1866. ∞ Six months later, McKenna was elected District Attorney for Solano County and served two terms. He practiced law and became increasingly active in politics. In 1875, McKenna was elected to the California House of Representatives and retired after one term and an unsuccessful bid for Speaker of the House. ∞ After two unsuccessful attempts, McKenna finally won election to the United States House of Representatives in 1885. He was re-elected three times. In 1892, President Benjamin Harrison appointed McKenna to the United States Court of Appeals for the Ninth Circuit. McKenna served in that position until he was appointed Attorney General of the United States by President William McKinley in 1897. ∞ On December 16, 1897, President McKinley nominated McKenna to the Supreme Court of the United States. The Senate confirmed the appointment on January 21, 1898. McKenna served on the Supreme Court for twenty-six years and retired on January 5, 1925. He died on November 21, 1926, at the age of eighty-three. ∞

OLIVER WENDELL HOLMES, JR.

Associate Justice 1902 – 1932

OLIVER WENDELL HOLMES, JR., was born on March 8, 1841, in Boston, Massachusetts. He was graduated from Harvard College in 1861. ∞ Holmes served for three years with the Massachusetts Twentieth Volunteers during the Civil War. He was wounded three times. In 1866 he returned to Harvard and received his law degree. The following year Holmes was admitted to the bar and joined a law firm in Boston, where he practiced for fifteen years. ∞ Holmes taught law at his alma mater, edited the American Law Review, and lectured at the Lowell Institute. In 1881, he published a series of twelve lectures on the common law, which was translated into several languages. ∞ In 1882, while working as a full professor at Harvard Law School, Holmes was appointed by the Governor to the Supreme Court of Massachusetts. He served on that Court for twenty years, the last three as Chief Justice. ∞ On December 2, 1902, President Theodore Roosevelt nominated Holmes to the Supreme Court of the United States. The Senate confirmed the appointment two days later. ∞ Holmes served on the Supreme Court for twenty-nine years and retired on January 12, 1932. He died on March 6, 1935, two days short of his ninety-fourth birthday. ∞

WILLIAM R. DAY

Associate Justice 1903 – 1922

WILLIAM R. DAY was born on April 17, 1849, in Ravenna, Ohio, and was graduated from the University of Michigan in 1870. After privately reading law for one year, Day studied law at the University of Michigan Law School for one year. He was admitted to the bar in 1872 and practiced law in Canton, Ohio, for the next twenty-five years. In 1886, Day was elected to the Court of Common Pleas in Canton but resigned after six months to return to his law practice. ∞ President William McKinley appointed Day First Assistant Secretary of State in 1897. On April 26, 1898, Day was elevated to Secretary. He served in that position until August 26, of that year, when he was appointed as a delegate to the Paris Peace Conference, which ended the Spanish-American War. ∞ In 1899, President McKinley appointed Day to the United States Court of Appeals for the Sixth Circuit. ∞ Four years later, on February 19, 1903, President Theodore Roosevelt nominated Day to the Supreme Court of the United States, and the Senate confirmed the appointment four days later. ∞ Day served on the Supreme Court for nineteen years. He retired on November 13, 1922, and accepted an appointment from President Warren G. Harding to serve on the Mixed Claims Commission to settle outstanding claims from World War I. Day died on July 9, 1923, at the age of seventy-four. ∞

WILLIAM H. MOODY

Associate Justice 1906 – 1910

WILLIAM H. MOODY was born in Newbury, Massachusetts, on December 23, 1853, and raised in nearby Danvers. He was graduated from Harvard College in 1876 and enrolled in Harvard Law School but left the Law School after one year to continue his legal studies with a Boston law firm. In 1878, he was admitted to the bar and established a law practice in Haverhill, Massachusetts. ∽ Ten years later, Moody was elected City Solicitor for Haverhill, and in 1890 he became District Attorney for the Eastern District of Massachusetts. In 1895, Moody won a special election to the United States House of Representatives and was re-elected three times. ∽ Moody resigned his House seat in 1902 to accept an appointment as Secretary of the Navy under President Theodore Roosevelt. From 1904 to 1906, he served as Attorney General of the United States. ∽ President Roosevelt nominated Moody to the Supreme Court of the United States on December 3, 1906. The Senate confirmed the appointment on December 12, 1906. ∽ Moody retired from the Supreme Court on November 20, 1910, after nearly four years of service. He died on July 2, 1917, at the age of sixty-three. ∽

HORACE H. LURTON

Associate Justice 1910 – 1914

ORACE H. LURTON was born in Newport, Kentucky, on February 26, 1844, and raised in Clarksville, Tennessee. He attended the University of Chicago in 1860 but joined the Confederate Army at the outbreak of the Civil War. Captured by Union soldiers, he soon escaped, but he was recaptured and released from prison just before the War ended. ∞ Lurton resumed his studies and was graduated from Cumberland University Law School in 1867. He returned to Clarksville and began the practice of law. In 1875, at the age of thirty-one, he was appointed by the Governor of Tennessee to the Sixth Chancery Division of Tennessee and became the youngest Chancellor in the history of the State. He resigned after three years and resumed his law practice. ∞ Lurton was elected to the Tennessee Supreme Court in 1886, and became its Chief Judge in 1893. Later that year, President Grover Cleveland appointed Lurton to the United States Court of Appeals for the Sixth Circuit, where he served for sixteen years. ∞ President William H. Taft nominated Lurton to the Supreme Court of the United States on December 13, 1909. The Senate confirmed the appointment one week later. ∞ Lurton served on the Supreme Court for four years. He died on July 12, 1914, at the age of seventy. ∞

WILLIS VAN DEVANTER

Associate Justice 1911 – 1937

ILLIS VAN DEVANTER was born on April 17, 1859, in Marion, Indiana. He received a law degree from the University of Cincinnati Law School in 1881 and joined his father's law firm in Marion. Three years later, Van Devanter moved to Cheyenne, Wyoming Territory, and established his own practice. ∞ Van Devanter served as a member of the commission that revised the statutes of the Wyoming Territory in 1886. In 1887, he served as City Attorney of Cheyenne, and in the following year he was elected to the Territorial Legislature. Van Devanter was only thirty years old when, in 1889, President Benjamin Harrison appointed him Chief Justice of the Wyoming Territorial Supreme Court. ∞ After Wyoming was admitted to the Union as the forty-fourth State in 1890, Van Devanter resigned as Chief Justice and returned to private practice. In 1897, President William McKinley appointed him an Assistant Attorney General, assigned to the Interior Department. President Theodore Roosevelt appointed him to the United States Court of Appeals for the Eighth Circuit in 1903. ∞ President William H. Taft nominated Van Devanter to the Supreme Court of the United States on December 12, 1910. The Senate confirmed the appointment three days later. Van Devanter served on the Supreme Court for twenty-six years. He retired on June 2, 1937, and died on February 8, 1941, at the age of eighty-one. ∞

JOSEPH RUCKER LAMAR

Associate Justice 1911 – 1916

JOSEPH RUCKER LAMAR was born in Ruckersville, Georgia, on October 14, 1857. He began his college education at the University of Georgia in 1874 and transferred one year later to Bethany College in West Virginia, where he was graduated in 1877. Lamar studied law at Washington and Lee University and clerked for an Augusta lawyer. He was admitted to the Georgia Bar in 1878. ∽ Lamar practiced law in Georgia from 1880 to 1910, with a few interruptions for public service. In 1886, he was elected to the Georgia Legislature, where he served two terms, and in 1893 the Governor appointed Lamar commissioner to codify Georgia laws. His work on the laws of Georgia was approved in 1895. ∽ Lamar was elected to the Georgia Supreme Court in 1903 but resigned in 1905 to return to private practice. ∽ President William H. Taft nominated Lamar to the Supreme Court of the United States on December 12, 1910. The Senate confirmed the appointment three days later. Lamar served on the Supreme Court for five years. He died on January 2, 1916, at the age of fifty-eight. ∽

MAHLON PITNEY
Associate Justice 1912 – 1922

MAHLON PITNEY was born on February 5, 1858, in Morristown, New Jersey. He was graduated from Princeton University in 1879 and earned a graduate degree three years later. Pitney studied law with his father and was admitted to the bar in 1882. ∞ Pitney practiced law for seven years in Dover, New Jersey. When his father was appointed Vice Chancellor of New Jersey in 1889, Pitney returned to Morristown and took over the elder Pitney's practice. ∞ Pitney was elected to the United States House of Representatives in 1894 and was re-elected in 1896. He resigned before the end of his second term when he was elected to the New Jersey State Senate. He was elected President of the Senate the following year. Pitney was appointed to the New Jersey Supreme Court for a seven-year term in 1901. In 1908, he was appointed Chancellor, head of both the law and equity branches of the Court. ∞ On February 19, 1912, President William H. Taft nominated Pitney to the Supreme Court of the United States. The Senate confirmed the appointment on March 13, 1912. Pitney retired from the Supreme Court on December 31, 1922, after ten years of service. He died on December 9, 1924, at the age of sixty-six. ∞

JAMES CLARK MCREYNOLDS

Associate Justice 1914 – 1941

JAMES CLARK MCREYNOLDS was born in Elkton, Kentucky, on February 3, 1862. He was graduated from Vanderbilt University in 1882, and from the University of Virginia Law School in 1884. ∞ McReynolds settled in Nashville, Tennessee, and established a law practice. He ran unsuccessfully for Congress in 1896. In 1900, McReynolds accepted a position as an adjunct Professor of Law at Vanderbilt University and taught there for three years. ∞ In 1903, President Theodore Roosevelt appointed McReynolds the Assistant Attorney General for the Antitrust Division in the Department of Justice. ∞ McReynolds resigned from the Department of Justice in 1907 to return to the practice of law, this time in New York, New York. In 1913, President Woodrow Wilson appointed him Attorney General of the United States. ∞ On August 19, 1914, President Wilson nominated McReynolds to the Supreme Court of the United States. The Senate confirmed the appointment on August 29, 1914. McReynolds retired from the Supreme Court on January 31, 1941, after twenty-six years of service. He died on August 24, 1946, at the age of eighty-four. ∞

LOUIS D. BRANDEIS
Associate Justice 1916 – 1939

Louis D. Brandeis was born in Louisville, Kentucky, on November 13, 1856. He attended preparatory school in Dresden, Germany, and was admitted to Harvard Law School in 1874. Following graduation in 1877, Brandeis moved to St. Louis, Missouri, where he practiced law. He returned to Cambridge, Massachusetts, and opened a law office with a law school classmate. ∞ During his career in private practice, Brandeis secured enactment of a state law providing low-cost insurance through savings banks, defended municipal control of Boston's subway system, and arbitrated labor disputes in the garment district of New York, New York. Brandeis was active in support of his alma mater and to civic affairs and was one of the founders of the *Harvard Law Review.* ∞ President Woodrow Wilson nominated Brandeis to the Supreme Court of the United States on January 28, 1916, and the Senate confirmed the appointment on June 1, 1916. He retired from the Supreme Court on February 13, 1939, after twenty-two years of service. He died on October 5, 1941, at the age of eighty-four. ∞

John H. Clarke

Associate Justice 1916–1922

John H. Clarke was born in Lisbon, Ohio, on September 18, 1857. Following graduation from Western Reserve College in 1877, he was tutored in law by his father and was admitted to the bar in 1878. ∞ After practicing law with his father's law firm for two years, Clarke moved to Youngstown, Ohio, and established his own practice, specializing in corporate law. He also acquired an ownership in the local newspaper, which was known for its support of progressive reform. He ran for the United States Senate in 1894 but was defeated by the incumbent. ∞ In 1897, Clarke left his practice in Youngstown to join a Cleveland law firm. ∞ Clarke had been a practicing attorney for thirty-five years when President Woodrow Wilson appointed him in 1914 to the United States District Court for the Northern District of Ohio, where he served for two years. ∞ On July 14, 1916, President Wilson appointed Clarke to the Supreme Court of the United States, and the Senate confirmed the appointment ten days later. ∞ Clarke resigned from the Supreme Court on September 18, 1922, to promote American participation in the League of Nations. He died on March 22, 1945, at the age of eighty-seven. ∞

GEORGE SUTHERLAND

Associate Justice 1922 – 1938

GEORGE SUTHERLAND was born in Buckinghamshire, England, on March 25, 1862. His family emigrated to America one year later and settled in Springville, Utah Territory. Sutherland studied at Brigham Young Academy in Provo, Utah, from 1878 to 1881, and attended the University of Michigan Law School for one year. ∞ Sutherland established a law practice in Provo, and after ten years moved to Salt Lake City. When Utah was admitted to the Union in 1896, Sutherland was elected to the first State Senate. Four years later, he was elected to the United States House of Representatives. In 1904, Sutherland was elected to the United States Senate and served two six-year terms. ∞ In 1921, President Warren G. Harding appointed Sutherland Chairman of the advisory committee to the Washington Conference on the Limitation of Naval Armaments. Sutherland also served as United States Consul at the Hague from 1921 to 1922. ∞ President Harding nominated Sutherland to the Supreme Court of the United States on September 5, 1922, and the Senate confirmed the appointment the same day. Sutherland retired on January 17, 1938, after fifteen years of service on the Supreme Court. He died on July 18, 1942, at the age of eighty. ∞

PIERCE BUTLER

Associate Justice 1923 – 1939

PIERCE BUTLER was born in Northfield, Minnesota, on March 17, 1866. He attended Carleton College and was graduated in 1887 with degrees in both arts and science. He moved to St. Paul and read law for one year at a law firm and was admitted to the bar in 1888. ∽ Three years later, Butler became an assistant county attorney of Ramsey County, which embraces the city of St. Paul. In 1893, he was elected County Attorney and served until 1897. ∽ While serving as County Attorney, Butler joined a law partnership and eventually became senior partner in a successor firm. In 1910, the Attorney General of the United States engaged Butler to represent the government in a number of antitrust cases. ∽ Butler served as a Regent of the University of Minnesota from 1907 to 1924. ∽ President Warren G. Harding nominated Butler to the Supreme Court of the United States on November 23, 1922. The Senate confirmed the appointment on December 21, 1922. ∽ Butler served on the Supreme Court for sixteen years and died on November 16, 1939, at the age of seventy-three. ∽

EDWARD T. SANFORD

Associate Justice 1923 – 1930

EDWARD T. SANFORD was born in Knoxville, Tennessee, on July 23, 1865. He was graduated from the University of Tennessee in 1883 and earned three degrees from Harvard University. Sanford then studied foreign languages and economics in France and Germany for one year. ∽ Sanford returned to Knoxville where he established a law practice. He was active in many educational, professional, and charitable organizations and also lectured in law at the University of Tennessee from 1898 to 1907. ∽ In 1906, Sanford became a Special Assistant to the Attorney General of the United States, with responsibility for prosecuting violations of the Sherman Antitrust Act of 1890. One year later, he was appointed an Assistant Attorney General of the United States. ∽ In 1908, President Theodore Roosevelt appointed Sanford to the United States District Court for the Middle and Eastern Districts of Tennessee, where he served for fifteen years. President Warren G. Harding nominated Sanford to the Supreme Court of the United States on January 24, 1923, and the Senate confirmed the appointment on January 29, 1923. Sanford served on the Supreme Court for seven years. He died on March 8, 1930, at the age of sixty-four. ∽

OWEN J. ROBERTS
Associate Justice 1930 – 1945

OWEN J. ROBERTS was born in Germantown, Pennsylvania, on May 2, 1875. He was graduated from the University of Pennsylvania in 1895 and received a law degree in 1898. Roberts was named a University Fellow in 1898 and taught in an adjunct capacity at the University of Pennsylvania until 1919. ∞ Roberts established a law practice in Philadelphia and served in a number of public offices. In 1901, he was appointed Assistant District Attorney in Philadelphia and served until 1904. In 1918, Roberts was appointed a Special Deputy Attorney General of the Eastern District of Pennsylvania. From 1924 to 1930, he served as a Special United States Attorney to investigate alleged wrongdoing in the Harding Administration. ∞ Roberts briefly returned to private practice in 1930, but on May 9, 1930, President Herbert Hoover nominated him to the Supreme Court of the United States. The Senate confirmed the appointment on May 20, 1930. ∞ While on the Court, Roberts oversaw an investigation into the attack on Pearl Harbor and headed a commission that traced art objects seized by the Germans in World War II. Roberts resigned from the Supreme Court on July 31, 1945, after fifteen years of service. He died on May 17, 1955, at the age of eighty. ∞

BENJAMIN NATHAN CARDOZO
Associate Justice 1932 – 1938

BENJAMIN NATHAN CARDOZO was born in New York, New York, on May 24, 1870. He was admitted to Columbia University at the age of fifteen, was graduated in 1889, and earned a graduate degree in 1890. Cardozo studied law at Columbia University and was admitted to the bar in 1891 before obtaining a degree. He began practicing appellate law with his older brother, and remained in private practice for twenty-three years. ∞ In 1914, Cardozo was elected to the New York Supreme Court, the state's trial bench. Later that year, the Governor of New York appointed him to a temporary position on the New York Court of Appeals. ∞ Cardozo was elected to a full term as an Associate Judge of the Court of Appeals in 1917, and in 1926 he became Chief Judge. His writings were used as a handbook for lawyers and his lectures at Yale Law School were expanded and published. ∞ On February 15, 1932, President Herbert Hoover nominated Cardozo to the Supreme Court of the United States. The Senate confirmed the appointment on February 24, 1932. ∞ Cardozo served on the Supreme Court for six years. He died on July 9, 1938, at the age of sixty-eight. ∞

HUGO BLACK

Associate Justice 1937 – 1971

Hugo L. Black was born in Harlan, Alabama, on February 27, 1886. He entered Birmingham Medical College in 1903, but after one year transferred to the University of Alabama Law School. He received his law degree in 1906. He was admitted to the bar and established a law practice in Ashland, Alabama. ∞ The following year, a fire destroyed his office and library, and Black moved to Birmingham. In 1911, he became a part-time police court judge, and in 1914 he was elected Public Prosecutor for Jefferson County. ∞ After military service in World War I, Black returned to his Birmingham law practice. In 1927, he was elected to the United States Senate and was re-elected six years later. ∞ In 1933, Black introduced legislation providing for a 30-hour work week which, as amended, became the Fair Labor Standards Act of 1938. ∞ President Franklin D. Roosevelt nominated Black to the Supreme Court of the United States on August 12, 1937, and the Senate confirmed the appointment five days later. ∞ Black retired from the Supreme Court on September 17, 1971, after thirty-four years of service. He died on September 25, 1971, at the age of eighty-five. ∞

STANLEY F. REED

Associate Justice 1938 – 1957

STANLEY F. REED was born in Minerva, Kentucky, on December 31, 1884. He was graduated from Kentucky Wesleyan University in 1902 and Yale University in 1906. After studying law at the University of Virginia and Columbia University, Reed took graduate courses in international law in Paris, France, in 1909 and 1910. ∞ Reed practiced law with a firm in Maysville, Kentucky, from 1910 to 1917, and served for four years in the Kentucky General Assembly. He went on active military duty in World War I, after which he returned to his law practice in Maysville. ∞ In 1929, President Herbert Hoover appointed Reed Counsel to the Federal Farm Board. Two years later, he was promoted to General Counsel of the Reconstruction Finance Corporation. In 1935, President Franklin D. Roosevelt appointed Reed Special Assistant to the Attorney General, and later that year Roosevelt appointed Reed Solicitor General of the United States. ∞ On January 15, 1938, President Roosevelt nominated Reed to the Supreme Court of the United States. The Senate confirmed the appointment on January 25, 1938. Reed retired from the Supreme Court on February 25, 1957, after nineteen years of service. After retirement, he served briefly as Chairman of President Dwight D. Eisenhower's Civil Rights Commission. He died on April 2, 1980, at the age of ninety-five. ∞

FELIX FRANKFURTER

Associate Justice 1939 – 1962

ELIX FRANKFURTER was born in Vienna, Austria, on November 15, 1882. When he was twelve years old, his family emigrated to the United States and settled in New York, New York. Frankfurter was graduated from the College of the City of New York in 1902 and Harvard Law School in 1906. ∞ Upon graduation, he took a position with a New York law firm, but within the year he was appointed an Assistant United States Attorney for the Southern District of New York. ∞ In 1910, Frankfurter began four years of service in the War Department's Bureau of Insular Affairs as a legal officer. In 1914, he accepted an appointment to the faculty of Harvard Law School. He returned to Washington in 1917 to become assistant to the Secretary of War. He later became Secretary and counsel to the President's Mediation Commission and, subsequently, Chairman of the War Labor Policies Board. After World War I he rejoined the Harvard Law School faculty. ∞ President Franklin D. Roosevelt nominated Frankfurter to the Supreme Court of the United States on January 5, 1939, and the Senate confirmed the appointment on January 17, 1939. After twenty-three years of service, Frankfurter retired from the Supreme Court on August 28, 1962. He died on February 22, 1965, at the age of eighty-two. ∞

WILLIAM O. DOUGLAS

Associate Justice 1939 – 1975

WILLIAM O. DOUGLAS was born in Maine, Minnesota, on October 16, 1898, and raised in Yakima, Washington. He entered Whitman College in 1916, but his studies were interrupted by military service in World War I. ∞ Douglas was graduated from Whitman in 1920 and taught school for two years before attending law school at Columbia University. Upon graduation in 1925, he joined a New York law firm, but left two years later to spend one year in Yakima. He subsequently returned to teach law at Columbia University, and transferred to the faculty of Yale University in 1929. ∞ In 1936, President Franklin D. Roosevelt appointed Douglas to the Securities and Exchange Commission, and in 1937 he became Chairman. ∞ President Roosevelt nominated Douglas to the Supreme Court of the United States on March 20, 1939. The Senate confirmed the appointment on April 4, 1939. ∞ Douglas had the longest tenure of any Justice, serving on the Supreme Court for thirty-six years with and spanning the careers of four Chief Justices. He retired on November 12, 1975, and died on January 19, 1980, at the age of eighty-one. ∞

FRANK W. MURPHY

Associate Justice 1940 – 1949

F RANK W. MURPHY was born on April 13, 1890, in Harbor Beach, Michigan. He was graduated from the University of Michigan in 1912 and University Law School in 1914. After his admission to the bar in 1914, Murphy clerked with a Detroit law firm for three years. In World War I, he served with the American forces in Europe. Murphy remained abroad after the War to pursue graduate studies in London and Dublin. ∞ In 1919, Murphy became Chief Assistant Attorney General for the Eastern District of Michigan, and from 1920 to 1923 he was engaged in private law practice. From 1923 to 1930, Murphy served on the Recorder's Court of Detroit. He was elected Mayor of Detroit in 1930 and served for three years. President Franklin D. Roosevelt appointed Murphy Governor General of the Philippines in 1933. When the Philippines achieved independence in 1935, Murphy was named United States High Commissioner. ∞ After his return to the United States in 1936, Murphy was elected Governor of Michigan and served for two years. President Roosevelt appointed him Attorney General of the United States in 1939. ∞ One year later, on January 4, 1940, President Roosevelt nominated Murphy to the Supreme Court of the United States. The Senate confirmed the appointment on January 15, 1940. Murphy served on the Supreme Court for nine years. He died on July 19, 1949, at the age of fifty-nine. ∞

JAMES F. BYRNES

Associate Justice 1941 – 1942

JAMES F. BYRNES was born in Charleston, South Carolina, on May 2, 1879. He left school at the age of fourteen to work as a law clerk in a Charleston law firm. He learned shorthand and became a court reporter in 1900. He then read law and was admitted to the bar in 1903. ∞ Byrnes became District Attorney for the Second Circuit of South Carolina in 1908, and in 1910 he was elected to the United States House of Representatives, where he served until 1925. In 1930 he was elected to the United States Senate, and he was re-elected in 1936. ∞ On June 12, 1941, President Franklin D. Roosevelt nominated Byrnes to the Supreme Court of the United States, and the Senate confirmed the appointment the same day. ∞ After only sixteen months of service, Byrnes resigned from the Supreme Court on October 3, 1942, to accept a series of wartime appointments. He served as Director, successively, of the Office of Economic Stabilization and the Office of War Mobilization. ∞ In 1945, President Harry S Truman appointed Byrnes Secretary of State. He resigned from that office in 1947, resumed the practice of law, and was elected Governor of South Carolina for a four-year term in 1950. Byrnes died on April 9, 1972, at the age of ninety-two. ∞

ROBERT H. JACKSON

Associate Justice 1941 – 1954

ROBERT H. JACKSON was born on February 13, 1892, in Spring Creek, Pennsylvania, and raised in Jamestown, New York. In 1912, he completed a two-year course of study at Albany Law School and served an apprenticeship in a law firm. He then established a law practice in Jamestown. ∞ In 1934, Jackson moved to Washington, D.C., to become General Counsel to the Internal Revenue Service. From 1936 to 1941, Jackson served successively as Assistant United States Attorney General, Solicitor General, and Attorney General of the United States. In the latter position, he devised the legal strategy by which President Franklin D. Roosevelt was able to provide destroyers to Great Britain in exchange for military bases on British territory. ∞ President Roosevelt nominated Jackson to the Supreme Court of the United States on June 12, 1941. The Senate confirmed the appointment on July 7, 1941. ∞ While on the Court, Jackson was appointed Chief United States Prosecutor at the International War Crimes Tribunal in Nuremberg, Germany. ∞ Jackson served on the Supreme Court for thirteen years. He died on October 9, 1954, at the age of sixty-two. ∞

WILEY B. RUTLEDGE

Associate Justice 1943 – 1949

ILEY B. RUTLEDGE was born in Cloverport, Kentucky, on July 20, 1894. During his early years, his family moved successively to Texas, Louisiana, and Asheville, North Carolina. Rutledge attended Maryville College in Tennessee for two years and transferred to the University of Wisconsin, from which he was graduated in 1914. He then taught high school and attended Indiana University Law School part-time. Rutledge received his law degree from the University of Colorado in 1922. ∞ Rutledge practiced law for two years with a firm in Boulder, Colorado, before deciding on an academic career. For the next fifteen years, he was a professor of law and dean at a succession of law schools. In 1935, he became Dean of the University of Iowa College of Law. In 1939, President Franklin D. Roosevelt appointed Rutledge to the United States Court of Appeals for the District of Columbia Circuit. ∞ Four years later, on January 11, 1943, President Roosevelt nominated Rutledge to the Supreme Court of the United States. The Senate confirmed the appointment on February 8, 1943. Rutledge served on the Supreme Court for six years. He died on September 10, 1949, at the age of fifty-five. ∞

HAROLD H. BURTON

Associate Justice 1945 – 1958

HAROLD H. BURTON was born in Jamaica Plain, Massachusetts, on June 22, 1888. He was graduated from Bowdoin College in 1909 and from Harvard Law School in 1912. ∽ After law school, Burton moved to Ohio, engaged in private practice for two years, and then worked for a public utility in Utah for two years. When the United States entered World War I, Burton was working as counsel for an Idaho public utility. He served in an infantry regiment of the United States Army, and at the end of the War returned to Cleveland and private law practice. ∽ Burton was elected to the Ohio House of Representatives in 1929 and the same year was named the Director of Law for the City of Cleveland. After serving a brief term as acting Mayor of Cleveland from 1931 to 1932, he was elected Mayor in 1935 and was twice re-elected. ∽ In 1941, Burton was elected to the United States Senate, where he served four years. ∽ President Harry S Truman nominated Burton to the Supreme Court on September 19, 1945, and the Senate confirmed the appointment the same day. ∽ Burton retired from the Supreme Court on October 13, 1958, after thirteen years of service. He died on October 28, 1964, at the age of seventy-six. ∽

TOM C. CLARK

Associate Justice 1949 – 1967

TOM C. CLARK was born on September 23, 1899, in Dallas, Texas. Following military service in World War I, Clark enrolled in the University of Texas, and received his law degree in 1922. ∞ Clark practiced law in Dallas until 1927, when he was appointed Civil District Attorney of the City. After serving five years he resumed his law practice. ∞ In 1937, Clark was appointed a Special Assistant in the Justice Department, and promoted to Assistant Attorney General in 1943. ∞ President Harry S Truman appointed Clark Attorney General of the United States in 1945, and he served in that position until 1949. On August 2, 1949, President Truman nominated Clark to the Supreme Court of the United States. The Senate confirmed the appointment on August 18, 1949. ∞ Clark served on the Supreme Court for seventeen years. He retired on June 12, 1967, when his son was appointed Attorney General of the United States. ∞ Following his retirement, Clark served as the first Chairman of the Federal Judicial Center, which was created by Congress to improve federal court administration. Clark also accepted assignments to sit by designation on various United States Courts of Appeals until his death on June 13, 1977, at the age of seventy-seven. ∞

SHERMAN MINTON

Associate Justice 1949 – 1956

SHERMAN MINTON was born in Georgetown, Indiana, on October 20, 1890. He received a law degree from Indiana University in 1915, where among his classmates were future Republican Presidential candidate, Wendell L. Willkie, and future Indiana Governor, Paul V. McNutt. Minton received an additional degree from Yale University Law School in 1917 following one year of graduate study. Minton established a law practice in New Albany, Indiana, a town near his birthplace. ∞ In 1933, Minton was appointed Public Counselor to the Indiana Public Service Commission. One year later, he ran successfully for the United States Senate and served one six-year term. In 1941, President Franklin D. Roosevelt appointed Minton to the White House staff as an administrative assistant in charge of coordinating military agencies. Later that year, President Roosevelt appointed Minton to the United States Court of Appeals for the Seventh Circuit, where he served eight years. ∞ President Harry S Truman nominated Minton to the Supreme Court of the United States on September 15, 1949. The Senate confirmed the appointment on October 4, 1949. ∞ Minton retired from the Supreme Court on October 15, 1956, after seven years of service. He died on April 9, 1965, at the age of seventy-four. ∞

John Marshall Harlan (II)

Associate Justice 1955 – 1971

JOHN MARSHALL HARLAN was born in Chicago, Illinois, on May 20, 1899, and named after his grandfather, who served as an Associate Justice from 1877 to 1911. Harlan was graduated from Princeton University in 1920 and studied law for three years at Balliol College, Oxford. He received his law degree from New York Law School in 1925. ∞ Harlan entered private practice with a New York law firm. He remained a member for twenty-five years but took periodic leaves of absence to serve in public office. In 1925, he was appointed an Assistant United States Attorney for the Southern District of New York, and from 1928 to 1930 he served as a Special Assistant Attorney General for New York. ∞ In World War II, Harlan served as an officer in the United States Air Force. After the War, he returned to his law practice and served as chief counsel to the New York State Crime Commission from 1951 to 1953. ∞ In 1954, President Dwight D. Eisenhower appointed Harlan to the United States Court of Appeals for the Second Circuit. On November 8, 1954, President Eisenhower nominated him to the Supreme Court of the United States. The Senate confirmed the appointment on March 16, 1955. ∞ Harlan retired from the Supreme Court on September 23, 1971. He died on December 29, 1971, at the age of seventy-two. ∞

WILLIAM J. BRENNAN, JR.

Associate Justice 1956 – 1990

WILLIAM J. BRENNAN, JR., was born on April 25, 1906, in Newark, New Jersey. He was graduated from the University of Pennsylvania in 1928 and received a law degree from Harvard University in 1931. ∞ After admission to the bar in 1932, Brennan joined a law firm and practiced until he began his military service in the Army with the outbreak of World War II and served as a member of the staff of the Under Secretary of War. When the War ended in 1945, he returned to Newark and resumed his law practice. ∞ In 1949, Governor Alfred E. Driscoll appointed Brennan to the newly created New Jersey Superior Court. The following year he was elevated to the Appellate Division of the Superior Court and two years later to the State Supreme Court. ∞ On October 16, 1956 President Dwight D. Eisenhower gave Brennan a recess appointment to the United States Supreme Court. Three months later, on January 14, 1957, Brennan was formally nominated to the Court, and the Senate confirmed the appointment on March 19, 1957. ∞ After thirty-three years of service, Brennan retired from the Supreme Court on July 20, 1990, at the age of eighty-four. ∞

CHARLES E. WHITTAKER

Associate Justice 1957 – 1962

CHARLES E. WHITTAKER was born in Troy, Kansas, on February 22, 1901. He left school at the age of sixteen to work on the family farm. Four years later, with tutoring, he was able to qualify for the University of Kansas City Law School and received a degree in 1924. He was admitted to the bar one year before his graduation. ∞ Whittaker joined the Kansas City law firm where he had worked part-time as an office boy during his student years and became a senior partner in two years. For the next thirty years, he practiced law. Whittaker was President of the Missouri Bar Association form 1953 to 1954. ∞ In 1954, President Dwight D. Eisenhower appointed Whittaker to the United States District Court for the Western District of Missouri. Two years later, President Eisenhower elevated him to the United States Court of Appeals for the Eighth Circuit. ∞ Whittaker had served for less than one year when, on March 2, 1957, President Eisenhower nominated him to the Supreme Court of the United States. The Senate confirmed the appointment on March 19, 1957. Whittaker served on the Supreme Court for five years. He retired on March 31, 1962, and died November 26, 1973, at the age of seventy-two. ∞

POTTER STEWART

Associate Justice 1958 – 1981

POTTER STEWART was born in Jackson, Michigan, on January 23, 1915. He was graduated from Yale College in 1937. After one year of postgraduate study at Cambridge University, England, he enrolled in Yale Law School. Following graduation in 1941, Stewart worked in a New York law firm. ∞ Stewart's legal career had just begun when the United States entered World War II. He served as an officer in the United States Navy and occasionally performed legal services in court-martials. After the War, he practiced law in New York, but soon returned to Cincinnati and joined a law firm there. ∞ Stewart practiced law in Cincinnati until 1954. He was twice elected to the City Council and served as Vice Mayor from 1952 to 1953. President Dwight D. Eisenhower appointed Stewart to the United States Court of Appeals for the Sixth Circuit in 1954, where he served for four years. ∞ On October 14, 1958, President Eisenhower gave Stewart a recess appointment to the Supreme Court of the United States. On January 17, 1959, Stewart was formally nominated to the Court, and the Senate confirmed the appointment on May 5, 1959. ∞ Stewart retired from the Supreme Court on July 3, 1981, after twenty-three years of service. He died on December 7, 1985, at the age of seventy. ∞

Byron R. White

Associate Justice 1962 –

Byron R. white was born in Fort Collins, Colorado, on June 8, 1917, and raised in the nearby town of Wellington. He entered the University of Colorado in 1934 and was graduated in 1938. White attended Oxford University as a Rhodes Scholar for one year and then enrolled in Yale Law School. ∞ White's education was interrupted by the United States entry into World War II. He joined the Navy, serving in the South Pacific. After the War, he completed his legal studies at Yale and was graduated in 1946. ∞ Upon graduation, White received an appointment as clerk to Chief Justice Fred M. Vinson of the United States Supreme Court for the 1946–1947 Term. He then returned to Colorado and practiced with a Denver law firm for fourteen years. ∞ In 1961, White was appointed Deputy Attorney General of the United States by President John F. Kennedy. White served in that position until March 30, 1962, when President Kennedy nominated him to the Supreme Court of the United States. The Senate confirmed the appointment on April 11, and White took the oath of office on April 16, 1962. ∞

ARTHUR J. GOLDBERG
Associate Justice 1962 – 1965

ARTHUR J. GOLDBERG was born in Chicago, Illinois, on August 8, 1908. He was graduated from Northwestern University in 1929 and received his law degree in 1930. ∞ Goldberg was admitted to the bar and joined a law firm in which he specialized in labor law. He first gained national recognition by representing the Chicago Newspaper Guild in a 1938 strike. Goldberg served as Chief of the Labor Division of the Office of Strategic Services in Europe during World War II. ∞ After the war, Goldberg returned to his practice and became counsel to both the Congress of Industrial Organizations and the United Steelworkers of America. He played a major role in the merger of the two largest national labor organizations in 1955. ∞ President John F. Kennedy appointed Goldberg Secretary of Labor in 1961. The following year, on August 29, 1962, President Kennedy nominated Goldberg to the Supreme Court of the United States, and the Senate confirmed the appointment on September 25, 1962. ∞ Goldberg had been on the Supreme Court for three years when, in 1965, President Lyndon B. Johnson appointed him United States Ambassador to the United Nations. Goldberg resigned from the Supreme Court on July 25, 1965. ∞ Goldberg retired from his ambassadorship in 1968 and returned to private practice. He died on January 19, 1990, at the age of eighty-one. ∞

ABE FORTAS

Associate Justice 1965 – 1969

ABE FORTAS was born in Memphis, Tennessee, on June 19, 1910. He was graduated from Southwestern College (now Rhodes University) in 1930 and from Yale University Law School in 1933. ∞ After graduation, Fortas taught law at Yale for one year. From 1934 to 1939, he held a series of positions in the newly created Securities and Exchange Commission. In the latter year, he became General Counsel to the Public Works Administration. ∞ In 1941, Fortas was appointed director of the division of power in the Department of the Interior, and one year later was named Under Secretary. ∞ Following World War II, Fortas and two associates established a law partnership in Washington, D.C., specializing in corporate law. ∞ After two decades of private practice, Fortas was appointed by President Lyndon B. Johnson to the Supreme Court of the United States on July 28, 1965. The Senate confirmed the appointment on August 11, 1965. ∞ Fortas served on the Supreme Court for three years. He resigned on May 14, 1969, and returned to private practice. He died on April 5, 1982, at the age of seventy-one. ∞

THURGOOD MARSHALL

Associate Justice 1967 – 1991

THURGOOD MARSHALL was born in Baltimore, Maryland, on July 2, 1908. He was graduated in 1930 from Lincoln University and in 1933 from Howard University Law School in Washington, D.C. ∞ Marshall began a legal career as counsel to the Baltimore Branch of the National Association for the Advancement of Colored People (NAACP). He joined the national legal staff in 1936 and in 1938 became Chief Legal Officer. ∞ In 1940, the NAACP created the Legal Defense and Education Fund, with Marshall as its Director and Counsel. For more than twenty years, Marshall coordinated the NAACP effort to end racial segregation. In 1954, he argued the case of *Brown* v. *Board of Education* before the Supreme Court of the United States. ∞ President John F. Kennedy appointed Marshall to the United States Court of Appeals for the Second Circuit in 1961. Four years later, President Lyndon B. Johnson appointed him Solicitor General of the United States. ∞ President Johnson nominated Marshall to the Supreme Court of the United States on June 13, 1967. The Senate confirmed the appointment on August 30, 1967. Marshall served twenty-three years on the Supreme Court, retiring on June 17, 1991, at the age of eighty-two. ∞

HARRY A. BLACKMUN

Associate Justice 1970 –

ARRY A. BLACKMUN was born in Nashville, Illinois, on November 12, 1908. He spent his early years in the St. Paul area of Minnesota. Blackmun was graduated from Harvard University in 1929 and Harvard Law School in 1932. ∞ Blackmun returned to Minnesota and served for one and a half years as a law clerk to Judge John B. Sanborn of the United States Court of Appeals for the Eighth Circuit, whom he succeeded on that Court more than twenty-five years later. ∞ In 1934, Blackmun entered private practice with a Minneapolis firm and remained there until 1950. During that time he served on the adjunct faculty at the University of Minnesota Law School and the St. Paul College of Law. In 1950, Blackmun became in-house counsel to the Mayo Foundation and Mayo Clinic in Rochester, Minnesota. ∞ President Dwight D. Eisenhower appointed Blackmun to the United States Court of Appeals for the Eighth Circuit in 1959. ∞ President Richard M. Nixon nominated Blackmun to the Supreme Court of the United States on April 14, 1970. The Senate confirmed the appointment on May 12, 1970. ∞

LEWIS F. POWELL, JR.

Associate Justice 1972 – 1987

LEWIS F. POWELL, JR., was born in Suffolk, Virginia, on September 19, 1907, and lived most of his life in Richmond, Virginia. He was graduated from Washington and Lee University in 1929 and from Washington and Lee University Law School in 1931. In 1932, he received a master's degree from Harvard Law School. ∞ Powell entered practice with a Richmond law firm, where he became a senior partner and continued his association until 1971. During World War II, he served in the United States Army Air Force in Europe and North America. ∞ After the War, Powell resumed his law practice. He served as the President of the American Bar Association from 1964 to 1965 and of the American College of Trial Lawyers from 1968 to 1969. In 1966, he served as a member of President Lyndon B. Johnson's Crime Commission. ∞ On October 21, 1971, President Richard M. Nixon nominated Powell to the Supreme Court of the United States. The Senate confirmed the appointment on December 6, 1971. Powell served on the Supreme Court for fifteen years. He retired on June 26, 1987, at the age of seventy-nine. ∞

John Paul Stevens

Associate Justice 1975 –

JOHN PAUL STEVENS was born in Chicago, Illinois, on April 20, 1920. He was graduated from the University of Chicago in 1941 and from Northwestern University School of Law in 1947, after having served in the United States Navy during World War II. He served as a law clerk to Associate Justice Wiley B. Rutledge of the United States Supreme Court for the 1947–1948 Term. ∞ He practiced law in Chicago from 1949 to 1970, except for 1951, when he served as Associate Counsel to the House Judiciary Committee's Subcommittee on the Study of Monopoly Power. In the early 1950s, Stevens taught on the law faculty at Northwestern and Chicago Universities. From 1953 to 1955, Stevens was a member of the Attorney General's National Committee to Study the Antitrust Laws. In 1969, he served as general counsel to a special commission appointed by the Illinois Supreme Court to investigate the integrity of one of its judgments. ∞ In 1970, President Richard M. Nixon appointed Stevens to the United States Court of Appeals for the Seventh Circuit. ∞ President Gerald R. Ford nominated Stevens to the Supreme Court of the United States on December 1, 1975. The Senate confirmed the appointment on December 17, 1975. ∞

Sandra Day O'Connor

Associate Justice 1981 –

Sandra day o'connor was born in El Paso, Texas, on March 26, 1930. She was graduated from Stanford University in 1950 and Stanford University Law School in 1952. After graduation, O'Connor became a Deputy County Attorney of San Mateo, California. She moved to Germany and worked as a civilian attorney for the United States Army in Frankfurt from 1954 to 1957. Upon her return to the United States, O'Connor engaged in private law practice. She was appointed to the Arizona State Senate in 1969 to fill an unexpired term, and the following year she was elected to the State Senate. Twice re-elected, she was majority leader of the State Senate from 1973 to 1974. O'Connor was elected to the Maricopa County Superior Court in 1975 and appointed to the Arizona Court of Appeals in 1979. President Ronald Reagan nominated O'Connor to the Supreme Court of the United States on August 19, 1981. The Senate confirmed the appointment on September 21, 1981, making O'Connor the first female Associate Justice in the history of the Court.

ANTONIN SCALIA

Associate Justice 1986 –

ANTONIN SCALIA was born on March 11, 1936, in Trenton, New Jersey, and raised in Queens, Long Island. He was graduated from Georgetown University in 1957, spending his junior year at the University of Fribourg, Switzerland. He was graduated from Harvard Law School in 1960. ∞ Scalia moved to Cleveland, Ohio, and practiced there until 1967, when he joined the faculty of the University of Virginia Law School. ∞ In 1971, Scalia became General Counsel of the White House Office of Telecommunications Policy. He was chairman of the Administrative Conference of the United States from 1972 to 1974. Scalia was appointed Assistant Attorney General of the Office of Legal Counsel in the Department of Justice in 1974. ∞ After one half year as Resident Scholar at the American Enterprise Institute in Washington, D.C., Scalia returned in 1977 to teaching at the University of Chicago Law School. He was also visiting professor at the Law Schools of Georgetown and Stanford Universities. ∞ President Ronald Reagan appointed Scalia to the United States Court of Appeals for the District of Columbia Circuit in 1982. Four years later, on June 24, 1986, President Reagan nominated Scalia to the Supreme Court of the United States. The Senate confirmed the appointment on September 17, 1986. ∞

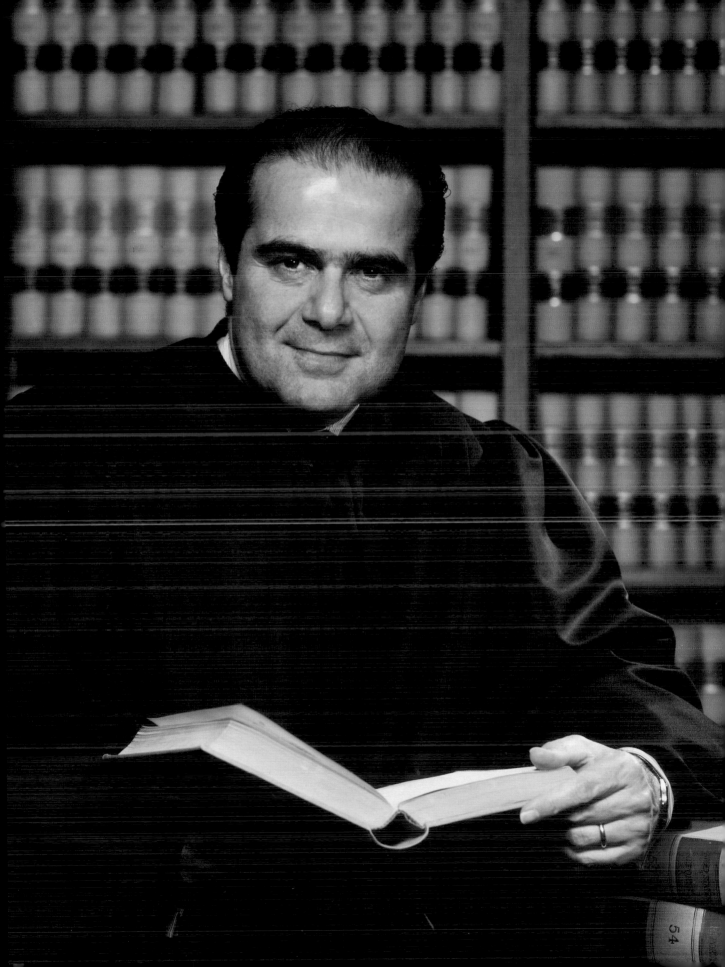

ANTHONY M. KENNEDY
Associate Justice 1988 –

ANTHONY M. KENNEDY was born in Sacramento, California, on July 23, 1936. While an undergraduate at Stanford University, Kennedy went to England to study at the London School of Economics for one year. He was graduated from Stanford University in 1958 and Harvard Law School in 1961. ∞ Kennedy was admitted to the California Bar in 1962 and practiced with a firm in San Francisco. One year later, he returned to his home town of Sacramento where he practiced law for twelve years. He also served as an adjunct professor at the McGeorge School of Law, University of the Pacific, from 1965 to 1988. ∞ In 1976, President Gerald Ford appointed Kennedy to the United States Court of Appeals for the Ninth Circuit, where he served for twelve years. While on that Court he served on the Board of Directors of the Federal Judicial Center. ∞ President Ronald Reagan nominated Kennedy to the Supreme Court of the United States on November 30, 1987. The Senate confirmed the appointment on February 3, 1988. ∞

DAVID H. SOUTER

Associate Justice 1990 –

DAVID H. SOUTER was born in Melrose, Massachusetts, on September 17, 1939. He was graduated from Harvard University in 1961. The following year he studied at Magdalen College, in Oxford, England, as a Rhodes Scholar. He was graduated from Harvard Law School in 1966. ∞ Souter was admitted to the bar and joined a law firm in Concord, New Hampshire. In 1968, he became an Assistant Attorney General of New Hampshire. In 1971, Souter became Deputy Attorney General and in 1976 Attorney General of the State of New Hampshire. During these years Souter also served on the New Hampshire Governor's Commission on Crime and Delinquency, the New Hampshire Judicial Council, the Maine–New Hampshire Interstate Boundary Commission, and the New Hampshire Policy Standards and Training Council. ∞ Souter became a Judge of the New Hampshire Superior Court in 1978. He was an Associate Justice of the New Hampshire Supreme Court from 1983 to 1990. ∞ President George Bush nominated Souter to the Supreme Court of the United States on July 15, 1990. The Senate confirmed the appointment on October 2, 1990. ∞

CLARENCE THOMAS
Associate Justice 1991 –

CLARENCE THOMAS was born in the Pinpoint community near Savannah, Georgia, on June 23, 1948. He was graduated from The College of the Holy Cross in 1971 and from Yale Law School in 1974. ∞ Thomas was admitted to the Missouri bar in 1974 and became an Assistant Attorney General of the State of Missouri the same year. He was an attorney for the Monsanto Company from 1977 to 1979. Thomas served as legislative assistant to Senator John C. Danforth of Missouri for the following two years. ∞ In 1981, Thomas was appointed Assistant Secretary for Civil Rights in the United States Department of Education. In 1982, he was named Chairman of the United States Equal Employment Opportunity Commission and served in that capacity until 1990. ∞ President George Bush appointed Thomas to the United States Court of Appeals for the District of Columbia Circuit in 1990. ∞ On July 1, 1991, President Bush nominated Thomas to the Supreme Court of the United States. The Senate confirmed the appointment on October 15, 1991. ∞

The Homes
of the Court

Since 1790, sessions of the Supreme Court have been held in a variety of locations and buildings. In fact, during its first 145 years, the Court held its hearings in 11 different locations.

ROYAL EXCHANGE, NEW YORK CITY
1790–1791

THE FIRST SESSION of the Court was held in the Royal Exchange building in New York City — the temporary capitol of the United States — across the street from the Fulton Fish Market. The building (which no longer exists) was located at the intersection of Broad and Water streets in what is now the financial district in lower Manhattan. The ground floor was a farmers' market and the Supreme Court hearing room on the second floor echoed with the cries of farmers hawking their produce and the bleating of animals. During these first two Terms, the Justices admitted lawyers to the bar and appointed a court crier and a clerk but heard no cases.

OLD CITY HALL, PHILADELPHIA
1791–1800

WHEN THE FEDERAL government moved the nation's capital to Philadelphia on February 7, 1791, the Supreme Court convened in Independence Hall. Although the court had no cases to hear, a number of lawyers presented themselves for admission to practice. In August 1791, the Court moved to the east wing of Philadelphia City Hall, which also housed the Pennsylvania State and Philadelphia Municipal Courts. These courts usually met at different times, but occasionally their schedules conflicted. Despite the fact that it was the highest court in the country, the Supreme Court often had to yield and meet on the second floor of the City Hall.

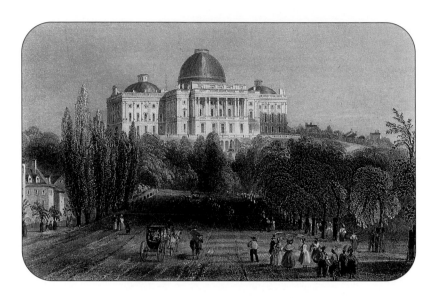

U.S. CAPITOL, WASHINGTON D.C.
1801–1814

THE FEDERAL CAPITAL moved to Washington, D.C. in 1801. Two weeks before the Court was scheduled to convene, it had not been assigned a place to meet. Congress passed a resolution to allow the Court a small room in the east basement of the unfinished Capitol. This was the first of a series of makeshift, hand-me-down quarters assigned to the Court. In February 1810, the Court met for the first time in a specially designed courtroom which it shared with the U.S. Circuit Court and the Orphan's Court of the District of Columbia. The Court remained in this room on the ground floor of the Capitol beneath the Senate Chamber until the Capitol was damaged by British troops during the War of 1812.

VARIOUS LOCATIONS, WASHINGTON D.C.
1815–1818

WHILE THE CAPITOL was being restored, the Supreme Court met in several
different locations in Washington. One site may have been this home on 204 B
Street, Southeast. In February 1817 the Court returned to an undestroyed section
in the north wing of the Capitol. These temporary quarters were described as
"mean and dingy" and "little better than a dungeon." The Court remained there
until the February 1819 Term, when reconstruction of its courtroom was completed.

SUPREME COURT CHAMBERS, U.S. CAPITOL
1819–1860

THE RESTORED COURTROOM in the Capitol, which the Justices were to occupy from 1819 to 1860, was the object of both praise and criticism. On its first hearing, The *National Intelligencer* reported "We are highly pleased to find that the Courtroom in the Capitol is in a state fit for the reception of the Supreme Court," while the *New York Statesman* said the room was "not in a style which comports with the dignity of that body or which bears a comparison with the other halls of the Capitol . . . . A stranger might traverse the dark avenues of the Capitol for a week without finding the remote corner in which Justice is administered to the American Republic."

OLD SENATE CHAMBERS, USED BY COURT, U.S. CAPITOL
1860–1935

IN 1860, the Court moved to the Old Senate Chamber on the first floor of the Capitol. The new courtroom, with several anterooms providing office space and storage, was the most spacious and ornate chamber the Supreme Court had been given in its first 70 years. The Justices sat on a raised platform behind a balustrade facing a large semi-circular colonnaded chamber. Despite the dignity of the courtroom, none of the Justices had individual office space in the Capitol, and each had to provide for his own working quarters. Moreover, the conference room where the Justices met to discuss cases also served as the Court library.

CONSTRUCTION OF THE SUPREME COURT
1932–1939

WILLIAM HOWARD TAFT, the only man to serve as both President and Chief Justice, began promoting the idea for a permanent building for the Court in 1912. Taft not only wanted adequate working conditions for the Justices but saw a separate building as symbolic of the independence of the Judicial Branch. At his persistent urging, Congress in 1929 authorized $9,740,000 for construction. Architect Cass Gilbert submitted plans for "a building of dignity and importance suitable for its use as a permanent home of the Supreme Court of the United States." Although Taft died in 1930 and Gilbert in 1934, the project was completed under Chief Justice Hughes in 1939.

THE SUPREME COURT, WASHINGTON D.C.
1935–PRESENT

THE SUPREME COURT held its first session in the new building at One First Street, Northeast, across from the Capitol, on October 7, 1935. Although the current building was not without its critics — one Justice is said to have compared the Supreme Court's new home to placing "nine black beetles in the Temple of Karnak" — most consider the monument a fitting tribute both to the importance of law in our system of government and to the principle of separation of powers that animates our constitutional democracy.

THE STRAIGHT BENCH

ON THE BENCH the Chief Justice occupies the center seat with the most senior Associate Justice seated to his right and the second senior Associate Justice seated to the Chief Justice's left. The remaining Associate Justices follow this pattern of alternating in order of seniority ending with the junior Justice seated at the Chief Justice's far left, at the end of the bench.

THE WINGED BENCH

IN 1972. the traditional straight bench was replaced by this more practical bench in three sections, providing the Justices with a view of the other members of the Court and enabling counsel to better hear questions from the bench.

A Ceremony at the Supreme Court

O<small>N</small> F<small>EBRUARY</small> 1, 1790, three members of the first Supreme Court met in a second floor room of the Royal Exchange Building in lower Manhattan. Lacking a quorum, the Justices adjourned until February 2 when a fourth justice arrived to make a quorum. The following remarks were made on January 16, 1990, at a ceremony at the Supreme Court in Washington, D.C., commemorating the bicentennial of that first sitting.

I HAVE ALWAYS BEEN PERSUADED THAT THE STABILITY

AND SUCCESS OF THE NATIONAL GOVERNMENT,

AND CONSEQUENTLY THE HAPPINESS

OF THE PEOPLE OF THE UNITED STATES,

WOULD DEPEND IN A CONSIDERABLE DEGREE

ON THE INTERPRETATION AND EXECUTION OF ITS LAWS.

IN MY OPINION, THEREFORE, IT IS IMPORTANT

THAT THE JUDICIARY SYSTEM

SHOULD NOT ONLY BE INDEPENDENT IN ITS OPERATIONS,

BUT AS PERFECT AS POSSIBLE IN ITS FORMATION.

G. WASHINGTON

TO CHIEF JUSTICE JAY AND ASSOCIATE JUSTICES, APRIL 3, 1790

Remarks

WARREN E. BURGER
Chief Justice of the United States 1969–1986

R. CHIEF JUSTICE, and may it please the Court: In a matter of days it will be 200 years since this Court first undertook to meet. On the first day, February 1, 1790, only three of the six Justices who had been confirmed were present. There being no quorum, they met the following day when the fourth Justice arrived. The fifth did not make it at all and the sixth, Justice Harrison, declined the appointment partly on the grounds of health and probably influenced by the reality that riding circuit, with the primitive conditions of travel in that day, was a burden that only a Justice in robust health could undertake.

As we know, this first session was held in a small room on the second floor of a small commercial building with an elaborate name — the Royal Exchange — in New York City across the street from the Fulton Fish Market near the waterfront. A bronze plaque was placed at this site by the American Bar Association in 1976.

Although the subject of Article III was extensively discussed at Philadelphia and in the ratification conventions, it did not receive the close attention, in some respects, that the other parts of the Constitution were given by the Committee on Style, where it might well have been noted that there was no reference to "Justices" in Article III but simply "judges." That was not consistent with the reference to the Office of Chief Justice in Article I assigning the duty to preside over impeachment trials. In the Judiciary Act of 1789, largely drafted by Senator Oliver Ellsworth, who would become the third Chief Justice, the office is described simply as "Chief Justice."

The structure of the federal system included a court of appeals to review the district courts, but it provided no judgeships for that court. It provided that those courts for each of the three circuits be made up of two Supreme Court Justices and one District Judge. Within a few years, the requirement of two Justices was reduced to one, but this still required Justices to ride circuit under great hardships of primitive travel and housing. In 1791, Chief Justice Jay urged that judgeships be provided for the circuit courts and the Congress did so in 1801 but then reversed itself in 1802.

In that day there seemed to be an attitude in the Congress that if the Justices of the Supreme Court were kept busy riding circuit they would be less troublesome to the other branches of government. Some members of Congress said just that. The history of that early period shows that in a good many instances judges of the state courts declined appointments to the Supreme Court largely because of the circuit riding burden. John Marshall had declined appointment several years before becoming Chief Justice.

Congress finally did respond to the urgings of President Washington and Chief Justice Jay and his successors by providing judges for the Court of Appeals and eliminating circuit riding burdens, but that was done, to borrow a phrase from English equity law, "with all deliberate speed." It was done in 1891.

There being no business before the Court in the first few sessions it undertook house keeping matters; it appointed a "cryer," adopted a seal for the Court and later appointed a clerk. At its second session it admitted some lawyers, and over the next two years it waited for the pipeline to bring some cases from the lower courts.

In the Court's first ten years there are fewer than 70 cases reported in the *U.S. Reports.* I suspect that members of the Court would like the docket to move in that direction — but without circuit riding.

The precise number of cases and opinions of the Court from 1790 to 1800 is not clear because apparently officers of the Court and those compiling the Reports may have decided that the records in some cases were not worth preserving. The records of those early years were not carefully kept and, of those that were kept, some were lost as the Court moved from New York to Philadelphia and then to Washington. Some were destroyed probably by the British when they occupied Washington in 1814. About 15 years ago the Court and the Historical Society joined in a project to reconstitute those records.

But it would be a mistake to assume that no important cases were decided in that first decade of the Court's history. Often overlooked, but possibly one of the most important, was the case of *Ware* v. *Hylton* argued in 1796 while the Court was sitting in Philadelphia, the only case John Marshall ever argued in this Court. The records indicate that the argument lasted about six days. *Ware* v. *Hylton* is important because it can be read as foreshadowing the holding in *Marbury* v. *Madison* seven years later. The Court held, as we know, that a treaty between the United States and

England terminating the war and requiring the payment of debts owed by Americans to British creditors be paid not in state currency but in the equivalent of "gold."

John Marshall lost the case in a unanimous holding of the Court, with Justice Samuel Chase writing the lead opinion and the other Justices writing separately, following the English custom.

I think Marshall as a judge would have decided *Ware* v. *Hylton* as the Court did. The best argument he could make was that the 1783 treaty did not apply and control the state legislative act because the debts were incurred before the Revolutionary War and before the Constitution. In holding that under Article VI, the treaty prevailed over a legislative act, *Ware* v. *Hylton* surely gave some hint of *Marbury*, but the opinion in it does not cite *Ware* v. *Hylton*. Whether that was because he wanted to forget about losing the case we have no way of knowing, but surely that great mind of his must have reasoned that if one clause of the Constitution controls over a legislative act the result in *Marbury* v. *Madison* was quite simple.

The young Supreme Court did not enjoy the prestige that it has today. It was not regarded as a co-equal branch, and some questioned whether it could survive. Even Chief Justice Jay, one of the greats among our founding fathers, did not see much of a future for the Court. He resigned after about six years to become governor of New York. After John Adams was defeated in the election of 1800 and Chief Justice Ellsworth resigned on the basis of health, Adams then offered the appointment to Jay. In declining he wrote that he would rather be governor of New York and, in any event, the Supreme Court as a tribunal would never amount to very much.

It was then that Adams, the lame duck President, turned to his Secretary of State, John Marshall, and invited him to take the appointment. Although Marshall had previously declined an appointment to this Court, he did accept and the year of 1801 began a great epoch in the history of this Court and of this country.

As we take note of this important anniversary of this Court — and of our country — it comes at the close of a decade when people all over the world are demanding the kinds of freedom this Court has been foremost in protecting for 200 years. Our history is their hope, and our hope for them must be that whatever systems they set up in place of the tyranny they have rejected will include a judiciary with authority and independence to enforce the basic guarantees of freedom, as this Court has done for these two hundred years. ∞

Remarks

REX E. LEE
Solicitor General of the United States 1981–1985

M R. CHIEF JUSTICE, and may it please the Court, I am honored to partici-
pate in this bicentennial commemoration, and specifically to make some
comments concerning the work of the Supreme Court bar over the 200 years
of the Court's history.

The clerk's familiar incantation, swearing new members of the bar as "attorneys and
counselors," is rooted in some interesting history. Originally, there was a distinction between the
two. The first rules of the Court, adopted on Thursday, February 5, 1790, provided that "counsellors shall not practice as attornies nor attornies as counsellors in this court." Historians tell us
the difference was that attorneys could file motions and do other paperwork, but only counselors
could "plead a case before the Court." The distinction lasted for eleven and one-half years, until
by rule adopted on August 12, 1801, the Court ordered "that Counsellors may be admitted as
Attornies in this Court, on taking the usual oath."

Over the two centuries of this Court's existence, there have stood before this podium
— or its equivalent in other parts of this town, in Philadelphia and New York — some very
able and prominent "attorneys and counselors." It is not surprising that appearances before
this Court during its early years were dominated by Attorneys General of the United States;
until the creation of the office of Solicitor General in 1870, it was the Attorney General who
was responsible for representing the United States before this Court. What is surprising is
that the most notable and most frequent appearances of those early Attorneys General were
not on behalf of the government but in representation of private clients. This was true of the
first Attorney General, Edmund Randolph, the second, William Bradford, the seventh, William Pinkney, and the ninth, William Wirt. Indeed, William Wirt, one of the greatest Supreme
Court advocates of all time and the man who holds the record for years of service as Attorney
General, confessed that "my single motive for accepting the office was the calculation of

being able to [obtain] more money for less work." Things were a little different then.

Edmund Randolph, our first Attorney General, was the most active of this Court's early practitioners. He appeared as counsel in the very first case (which came up during the February 1791 term) *Van Staphorst and Van Staphorst v. Maryland.* He also argued the first landmark case, *Chisholm v. Georgia.* Indeed, he was the only person who argued in that case. The state of Georgia refused to appear, and at the conclusion of Randolph's argument, which lasted two and one-half hours, the Court's minutes reflect that "the Court, after remarking on the importance of the subject now before them . . . expressed the wish to hear any gentlemen of the bar who might be disposed to take up the gauntlet in opposition to the Attorney General. As no gentlemen, however, were so disposed, the Court held the matter under advisement . . . ." It would appear that the rules governing oral argument by *amici* were a bit more liberal in those days.

The same is true of divided arguments, time limits, and questions from the bench. Representing the two sides in the oral argument in *McCulloch v. Maryland* was perhaps the greatest collection of prominent advocates in the history of this Court's bar. Arguing for the bank were William Pinkney, William Wirt, and Daniel Webster. And representing Maryland were Luther Martin, Joseph Hopkinson, and Walter Jones. The entire argument, by all six counsel, lasted nine days; Thomas Edison's birth was still twenty-eight years away, and there were no red nor white lights. Those were the days when there were no questions; both the commentators and the advocates themselves referred to their arguments as speeches, which they would rehearse for days. Charles Warren relates that "the social season of Washington began with the opening of the Supreme Court term," and some of those early lawyers, particularly Webster and Pinkney, apparently responded by paying as much attention to the gallery as to the justices.

Pinkney's argument alone in *McCulloch* lasted for three full days. It was a performance which Professor Warren has said "was to prove the greatest effort of his life . . . ." Pinkney was described by Chief Justice Marshall as "the greatest man [he] had ever seen in a court of justice"; by Chief Justice Taney as one to whom there was "none equal"; by Justice Story as having "great superiority over every other man [he had] ever known"; and by Francis Wheaton as the "brightest and meanest of mankind."

Pinkney had the distinction of serving as Attorney General of both the United States and also the state of Maryland, as a member of both Houses of Congress, and minister to Great

Britain and Russia. But whichever of these was paramount, it was in Pinkney's view a distant second to his one consuming passion: advocate before this Court. It was an endeavor to which he gave his life, both figuratively and literally. Following the completion of the last of his eighty-four arguments, in *Ricard* v. *Williams* — in 1822 with Daniel Webster on the other side — he suffered a collapse. He was carried to his home, where he died a few days later. Incidentally, he lost *Ricard* v. *Williams,* an unpleasant experience for any lawyer, but one that is well-known to those who are seasoned.

Walter Jones holds the record number of oral arguments with 317. It is a record which, given today's realities, is surely safe for all time. For Mr. Jones, there will be no Roger Maris or Hank Aaron. Daniel Webster is in second place, and it would appear that John W. Davis is third, and Erwin Griswold fourth. But the record number of landmarks, in my opinion, belongs to William Wirt, whose biographer has accurately observed that "he appeared in virtually all of the landmark cases of the first third of the nineteenth century." These included *Dartmouth College* v. *Woodward, McCulloch* v. *Maryland, Cohens* v. *Virginia, Gibbons* v. *Ogden, Brown* v. *Maryland, Ogden* v. *Saunders, Worcester* v. *Georgia, Cherokee Nation* v. *Georgia,* and *Charles River Bridge* v. *Warren Bridge.* Wirt was described by Chief Justice Chase as "one of the purest and noblest of men" and by another contemporary as "the most beloved of American advocates."

In four of these landmarks, *Dartmouth College, McCulloch, Cohens* v. *Virginia,* and *Gibbons* v. *Ogden,* Wirt appeared with Daniel Webster. They argued *Dartmouth College* and *McCulloch* just three weeks apart. He was the Attorney General at the time, and though in *McCulloch* he was arguing to sustain the power of the federal government, he received a substantial fee from the Bank of the United States.

Daniel Webster, though he won slightly less than half of his cases, probably had the greatest influence on the Court and its work of any nineteenth century advocate — perhaps the greatest influence of any advocate in the Court's history. S. W. Finley has observed that "Webster and Chief Justice Marshall shared the same basic constitutional philosophy, and together with Justice Joseph Story they constitute a fortuitous triumvirate in establishing the fundamentals of American federalism in the first four decades of the nineteenth century."

The twentieth century, of course, is not yet complete, but it is already clear that during the Court's second hundred years, advocates to match the stature of Pinkney, Wirt, and Webster have stood at this podium. Comparisons are difficult because of changes in circumstances and rules, but quite clearly the Court's jurisprudence during this century has been influenced by people such as John W. Davis, Robert Jackson, Thurgood Marshall, and Erwin Griswold, just as it was during earlier times by Pinkney, Wirt, and Webster. And our century also has had its equivalent of *McCulloch*'s battle of the giants when, for example, *Briggs* v. *Elliot,* a companion case to *Brown* v. *Board of Education,* pitted John W. Davis against Thurgood Marshall.

Mr. Chief Justice, we the members of the bar of this Court are proud of the institution whose two hundredth birthday we celebrate, proud of what it has meant and what it has done for our country and its people, and proud of the contribution that the members of the bar have made to the Court and its accomplishments over its two-hundred-year history. We recognize that we are more than attorneys and counselors. As officers of the Court, we are charged not only with the responsibility of vigorously representing our clients but also assuring that our representation is objective, fair, evenhanded, and contributory to the Court's performance of its duties. We are mindful of the institution before which we practice, and the role that it has played from 1790 to 1990 in securing individual rights and providing stable government. We are pleased to offer our continuing services as we enter the Court's third century. ❧

Remarks

KENNETH W. STARR

Solicitor General of the United States 1989–

ALMOST HALF A CENTURY after this Court's opening session, Alexis de Tocqueville, the French observer of democracy in the new Republic, turned his eye back to the Founding Fathers and saw in that remarkable generation the finest minds and noblest characters ever to have graced the New World.

And the wisest, ablest minds of that generation were well represented in the membership of this Court. As we have been reminded, the docket may not have been especially demanding, and the rigors of office may have been daunting, but the Court nonetheless boasted among its members not only its distinguished Chief Justice, John Jay, author along with Madison and Hamilton of *The Federalist Papers,* but also several delegates to the Constitutional Convention itself. Like the Nation's first Attorney General, Edmund Randolph of Virginia (whose successor is here today), Justices Rutledge of South Carolina, Wilson of Pennsylvania, and Blair of Virginia had served as members of the Convention. Other Justices of the 1790s, including Iredell of North Carolina and Cushing of Massachusetts, had played pivotal roles in their respective States in securing ratification.

To these individuals, along with their counterparts in the political branches, fell the task of forming a workable government. It was John Jay who articulated the basic structural insight:

> "Wise and virtuous men have thought and reasoned very differently respecting Government, but in this they have at length very unanimously agreed. That its powers should be divided into three, distinct, independent Departments — the Executive legislative and judicial."

As Providence would have it, in our system of separated powers, it fell in no small measure to the Court to serve as an instrument of achieving the Madisonian and Hamiltonian vision of a vast commercial republic. That was not without difficulty, since this was to be the branch where, as Hamilton put it, judgment, not will, was to be exercised.

The fundamental importance of the judgment of the judiciary was made manifest early on. That our constitutional democracy, by virtue of the status of the Constitution as supreme law, would include the power of judicial review was evidenced in the judicial literature as early as 1792 in *Hayburn's Case*. If not before, the decision of *Hylton* v. *United States* in 1796, upholding the constitutionality of the federal Carriage Tax, powerfully foreshadowed *Marbury* v. *Madison*. In short, although the judiciary was to be the least dangerous branch, it was nonetheless to be a truly co-equal, coordinate branch with the Legislature and the Executive.

In view of the Court's role, friction between the federal judiciary and the several States was inevitable, just as leading Anti-Federalists such as George Mason had pessimistically predicted. Quite apart from *Chisholm* v. *Georgia*, other decisions of that first decade now dim in the national memory made clear that the national power in its proper sphere extended to and ultimately controlled the States. This was important to be said, and the Court did not flinch from saying it.

These formative principles — of the legitimacy as well as the limits of judicial power, and of the need to vindicate the primacy of the Nation in its appropriate sphere over narrow, parochial interests — provided important grist for the early judicial mill. Along with Washington's stewardship of the Executive power, and the wisdom of the first Congress — graced by Madison himself, who turned his hand to fashioning the Bill of Rights — the leaders of the Nation in all three branches brought to life in 1789 and 1790 what the Framers had envisioned — a balanced government, destined to stand the test of time.

The Nation has endured and prospered. The structure of government has endured. The Court has endured. And with the long-sought abolition of slavery, the promise of legal equality — embodied in the 14th Amendment — took root and grew so that the original vision of the Declaration and the Constitution's vision of a more perfect union, preserved out of bitter conflict, and a true constitutional democracy for all our citizens came fully to life. It was in large measure these events — so important for the work of this Court over the past century — that brought the Department of Justice into being in the wake of the Civil War.

This was what Tocqueville had seen so clearly, peering as he did into the future, looking at us with prophetic vision. Social equality, as Tocqueville put it, was what America ultimately promised through the emergence of democratic institutions. This was, he felt, the will of God. From the American experience, purified by slavery's inevitable eradication, Tocqueville believed that Europe could learn and morally profit. This was a new order of the ages. Out of the mouths of babes in the New World, truths about what the Twentieth Century moral imagination of T. S. Eliot would call, simply, the permanent things, would emerge — the moral vision of equal justice under the rule of law. This was, as demonstrated by events now unfolding across the globe, a powerful vision destined to capture the moral imagination of the entire family of mankind.

For that vision brought to life in the judiciary's daily, steadfast service to the law, those of us privileged to serve in the Department of Justice, under the stewardship of the officer whose office was created by the Judiciary Act of 1789, salute the courts of Justice and the tribunal ordained in Article III of our beloved Constitution as "one supreme Court." As Lincoln put it so simply at Gettysburg, only seven years before the birth of our own Department, it is entirely fitting and proper that should we do this.

Remarks

WILLIAM H. REHNQUIST
Chief Justice of the United States 1986–

CHIEF JUSTICE BURGER, General Starr, Mr. Lee: your felicitous remarks have shown how the Supreme Court of the United States got off to what was indeed a slow start in New York two hundred years ago, but eventually picked up the necessary speed to evolve into a truly co-equal branch of the federal government.

Half a century ago the Court held a ceremony similar to this one, commemorating the one hundred and fiftieth anniversary of its first session. Attorney General Robert H. Jackson — soon himself to become a member of this Court — addressed the Court on that occasion, saying:

> "[T]his age is one of founding fathers to those who follow. Of course, they will reexamine the work of this day, and some will be rejected. Time will no doubt disclose that sometimes when our generation thinks it is correcting a mistake of the past, it is really only substituting one of its own . . . . I see no reason to doubt that the problems of the next half-century will test the wisdom and courage of this Court as severely as any half-century of its existence."

None of us here today can doubt the accuracy of Robert Jackson's assessment of this Court's succeeding half-century. All of us realize how significantly — indeed, how dramatically — the interpretation of the United States Constitution has changed in the past fifty years. And yet, we, too, must realize that our work has no more claim to infallibility than that of our predecessors. Daniel Webster said that "Justice is the great interest of man on earth" — a statement which attests his wisdom not only as a statesman but as a theologian — and the motto inscribed on the front of this building — "Equal Justice Under Law" — describes a quest, not a destination.

But if we look at the temporal context of the ceremony here in this room fifty years ago, it was vastly different from the one today. The gathering storm of war had burst a few months earlier with the German invasion of Poland. A few months later the German breakthrough in the Ardennes would knock France out of the war, leaving Great Britain and her commonwealth allies fighting alone against the dictators. The fate of constitutional ideals such as self-government and the rule of law seemed to hang in the balance of war.

How different it is today. The allies won the Second World War, and the worth of western values was reestablished. In February 1940, when this Court celebrated its one hundred and fiftieth anniversary, it was virtually the only constitutional court — a court whose existence was based on a written constitution which had the authority to invalidate legislative acts — sitting anywhere in the world. But after the Second World War, the idea of such a court found favor with nation after nation.

The written Constitution drafted by the framers in Philadelphia in 1787 incorporated two ideas which were new to the art of government. The first is the system of presidential government, in which the executive authority was separated from the legislative authority. This idea has found little favor outside the United States, and countries just as committed to democratic self-government as we are have preferred the parliamentary system.

The second idea was that of a constitutional court which should have authority to enforce the provisions of a written constitution. It is this second idea which has commended itself to country after country following the Second World War. Today its momentum continues. Less than a decade ago Canada adopted a charter of rights to be enforced by its Supreme Court. In countries today which do not have a full-scale constitutional court — Great Britain, Sweden, Australia — proponents of change are engendering lively debate. I do not think that I overstate the case when I say that the idea of a constitutional court such as this one is the most important single American contribution to the art of government.

As we look today toward eastern Europe, where a curtain which had been drawn for nearly half of a century has been lifted only within the past year — it may not be too much to hope that these nations, too, will see fit to reshape their judiciaries on the American model.

The three Justices who gathered in New York City on February 1, 1790, could not possibly have foreseen the future importance of the court upon which they accepted the call to serve. I am confident that even those who gathered here fifty years ago could not have foreseen the changes and developments in the law which would come in the next half-century, nor the influence that this institution would have outside its borders during that time. And surely the same is true of those of us who have gathered here today to commemorate the bicentennial of the Court's first sitting.

We have no way of knowing with certainty where the quest for equal justice under law will lead our successors in the next half-century. If at times our labors seem commonplace or even unavailing, let us hark to the words of Arthur Hughe Clough:

> And not by eastern windows only
> When daylight comes, comes in the light
> In front the sun climbs slow, how slowly
> But westward look, the land is bright! ∞

MEMBERS OF
THE SUPREME COURT

CHIEF JUSTICES	Place of Birth	Date of Birth	State Appointed From	Appointed by President
John Jay	New York	Dec. 12, 1745	New York	Washington
John Rutledge	S. Carolina	Sept. 1739	S. Carolina	Washington
Oliver Ellsworth	Connecticut	Apr. 29, 1745	Connecticut	Washington
John Marshall	Virginia	Sept. 24, 1755	Virginia	Adams, John
Roger Brooke Taney	Maryland	Mar. 17, 1777	Maryland	Jackson
Salmon Portland Chase	New Hampshire	Jan. 13, 1808	Ohio	Lincoln
Morrison R. Waite	Connecticut	Nov. 29, 1816	Ohio	Grant
Melville Weston Fuller	Maine	Feb. 11, 1833	Illinois	Cleveland
Edward Douglass White	Louisiana	Nov. 3, 1845	Louisiana	Taft
William Howard Taft	Ohio	Sept. 15, 1857	Connecticut	Harding
Charles Evans Hughes	New York	Apr. 11, 1862	New York	Hoover
Harlan Fiske Stone	New Hampshire	Oct. 11, 1872	New York	Roosevelt, F.
Fred M. Vinson	Kentucky	Jan. 22, 1890	Kentucky	Truman
Earl Warren	California	Mar. 19, 1891	California	Eisenhower
Warren E. Burger	Minnesota	Sept. 17, 1907	Virginia	Nixon
William H. Rehnquist	Wisconsin	Oct. 1, 1924	Virginia	Reagan

(A) Judicial Oath Taken	(B) Age Oath Taken	Date Service Terminated	Service Terminated By	(B) Years of Service	(B) Age at End of Term	Date of Death	(B) Age at Death
Oct. 19, 1789	43	June 29, 1795	Resignation	5	49	May 17, 1829	83
Aug. 12, 1795	55	Dec. 15, 1795	Rejection	(C) 0	56	July 18, 1800	60
Mar. 8, 1796	50	Dec. 15, 1800	Resignation	4	55	Nov. 26, 1807	62
Feb. 4, 1801	45	July 6, 1835	Death	34	79	July 6, 1835	79
Mar. 28, 1836	59	Oct. 12, 1864	Death	28	87	Oct. 12, 1864	87
Dec. 15, 1864	56	May 7, 1873	Death	8	65	May 7, 1873	65
Mar. 4, 1874	57	Mar. 23, 1888	Death	14	71	Mar. 23, 1888	71
Oct. 8, 1888	55	July 4, 1910	Death	21	77	July 4, 1910	77
Dec. 19, 1910	65	May 19, 1921	Death	(C) 10	75	May 19, 1921	75
July 11, 1921	63	Feb. 3, 1930	Retirement	8	72	Mar. 8, 1930	72
Feb. 24, 1930	67	July 1, 1941	Retirement	(C) 11	79	Aug. 27, 1948	86
July 3, 1941	68	Apr. 22, 1946	Death	(C) 4	73	Apr. 22, 1946	73
June 24, 1946	56	Sept. 8, 1953	Death	7	63	Sept. 8, 1953	63
Oct. 5, 1953	62	June 23, 1969	Retirement	15	78	July 9, 1974	83
June 23, 1969	61	Sept. 26, 1986	Retirement	17	79		
Sept. 26, 1986	61			(C)			

ASSOCIATE JUSTICES	Place of Birth	Date of Birth	State Appointed From	Appointed by President
James Wilson	Scotland	Sept. 14, 1742	Pennsylvania	Washington
William Cushing	Massachusetts	Mar. 1, 1732	Massachusetts	Washington
John Blair, Jr.	Virginia	1732	Virginia	Washington
John Rutledge	S. Carolina	Sept. 1739	S. Carolina	Washington
James Iredell	England	Oct. 5, 1751	N. Carolina	Washington
Thomas Johnson	Maryland	Nov. 4, 1732	Maryland	Washington
William Paterson	Ireland	Dec. 24, 1745	New Jersey	Washington
Samuel Chase	Maryland	Apr. 17, 1741	Maryland	Washington
Bushrod Washington	Virginia	June 5, 1762	Virginia	Adams, John
Alfred Moore	N. Carolina	May 21, 1755	N. Carolina	Adams, John
William Johnson	S. Carolina	Dec. 17, 1771	S. Carolina	Jefferson
H. Brockholst Livingston	New York	Nov. 25, 1757	New York	Jefferson
Thomas Todd	Virginia	Jan. 23, 1765	Kentucky	Jefferson
Gabriel Duvall	Maryland	Dec. 6, 1752	Maryland	Madison
Joseph Story	Massachusetts	Sept. 18, 1779	Massachusetts	Madison
Smith Thompson	New York	Jan. 17, 1768	New York	Monroe
Robert Trimble	Virginia	Nov. 17, 1776	Kentucky	Adams, J. Q.
John McLean	New Jersey	Mar. 11, 1785	Ohio	Jackson
Henry Baldwin	Connecticut	Jan. 14, 1780	Pennsylvania	Jackson
James M. Wayne	Georgia	1790	Georgia	Jackson
Philip P. Barbour	Virginia	May 25, 1783	Virginia	Jackson
John Catron	Pennsylvania	1786	Tennessee	Jackson
John McKinley	Virginia	May 1, 1780	Alabama	Van Buren
Peter V. Daniel	Virginia	Apr. 24, 1784	Virginia	Van Buren

(A) Judicial Oath Taken	(B) Age Oath Taken	Date Service Terminated	Service Terminated By	(B) Years of Service	(B) Age at End of Term	Date of Death	(B) Age at Death
Oct. 5, 1789	47	Aug. 21, 1798	Death	8	55	Aug. 21, 1798	55
Feb. 2, 1790	57	Sept. 13, 1810	Death	20	78	Sept. 13, 1810	78
Feb. 2, 1790	58	Jan. 27, 1796	Resignation	5	64	Aug. 31, 1800	68
Feb. 15, 1790	50	Mar. 5, 1791	Resignation	1	51	July 18, 1800	60
May 12, 1790	38	Oct. 20, 1799	Death	9	48	Oct. 20, 1799	48
Aug. 6, 1792	59	Jan. 16, 1793	Resignation	0	60	Oct. 26, 1819	86
Mar. 11, 1793	47	Sept. 9, 1806	Death	13	60	Sept. 9, 1806	60
Feb. 4, 1796	54	June 19, 1811	Death	15	70	June 19, 1811	70
Feb. 4, 1799	36	Nov. 26, 1829	Death	30	67	Nov. 26, 1829	67
Apr. 21, 1800	45	Jan. 26, 1804	Resignation	3	48	Oct. 15, 1810	55
May 7, 1804	32	Aug. 4, 1834	Death	30	62	Aug. 4, 1834	62
Jan. 20, 1807	49	Mar. 18, 1823	Death	16	65	Mar. 18, 1823	65
May 4, 1807	42	Feb. 7, 1826	Death	18	61	Feb. 7, 1826	61
Nov. 23, 1811	58	Jan. 14, 1835	Resignation	23	82	Mar. 6, 1844	91
Feb. 3, 1812	32	Sept. 10, 1845	Death	33	65	Sept. 10, 1845	65
Sept. 1, 1823	55	Dec. 18, 1843	Death	20	75	Dec. 18, 1843	75
June 16, 1826	49	Aug. 25, 1828	Death	2	51	Aug. 25, 1828	51
Jan. 11, 1830	44	Apr. 4, 1861	Death	31	76	Apr. 4, 1861	76
Jan. 18, 1830	50	Apr. 21, 1844	Death	14	64	Apr. 21, 1844	64
Jan. 14, 1835	45	July 5, 1867	Death	32	77	July 5, 1867	77
May 12, 1836	52	Feb. 25, 1841	Death	4	57	Feb. 25, 1841	57
May 1, 1837	51	May 30, 1865	Death	28	79	May 30, 1865	79
Jan. 9, 1838	57	July 19, 1852	Death	14	72	July 19, 1852	72
Jan. 10, 1842	57	May 31, 1860	Death	18	76	May 31, 1860	76

ASSOCIATE JUSTICES	Place of Birth	Date of Birth	State Appointed From	Appointed by President
Samuel Nelson	New York	Nov. 10, 1792	New York	Tyler
Levi Woodbury	New Hampshire	Dec. 22, 1789	New Hampshire	Polk
Robert C. Grier	Pennsylvania	Mar. 5, 1794	Pennsylvania	Polk
Benjamin R. Curtis	Massachusetts	Nov. 4, 1809	Massachusetts	Fillmore
John A. Campbell	Georgia	June 24, 1811	Alabama	Pierce
Nathan Clifford	New Hampshire	Aug. 18, 1803	Maine	Buchanan
Noah H. Swayne	Virginia	Dec. 7, 1804	Ohio	Lincoln
Samuel F. Miller	Kentucky	Apr. 5, 1816	Iowa	Lincoln
David Davis	Maryland	Mar. 9, 1815	Illinois	Lincoln
Stephen J. Field	Connecticut	Nov. 4, 1816	California	Lincoln
William Strong	Connecticut	May 6, 1808	Pennsylvania	Grant
Joseph P. Bradley	New York	Mar. 14, 1813	New Jersey	Grant
Ward Hunt	New York	June 14, 1810	New York	Grant
John Marshall Harlan	Kentucky	June 1, 1833	Kentucky	Hayes
William B. Woods	Ohio	Aug. 3, 1824	Georgia	Hayes
Stanley Matthews	Ohio	July 21, 1824	Ohio	Garfield
Horace Gray	Massachusetts	Mar. 24, 1828	Massachusetts	Arthur
Samuel Blatchford	New York	Mar. 9, 1820	New York	Arthur
Lucius Q. C. Lamar	Georgia	Sept. 17, 1825	Mississippi	Cleveland
David J. Brewer	Asia Minor	June 20, 1837	Kansas	Harrison, B.
Henry B. Brown	Massachusetts	Mar. 2, 1836	Michigan	Harrison, B.
George Shiras, Jr.	Pennsylvania	Jan. 26, 1832	Pennsylvania	Harrison, B.
Howell E. Jackson	Tennessee	Apr. 8, 1832	Tennessee	Harrison, B.
Edward Douglass White	Louisiana	Nov. 3, 1845	Louisiana	Cleveland

(A) Judicial Oath Taken	(B) Age Oath Taken	Date Service Terminated	Service Terminated By	(B) Years of Service	(B) Age at End of Term	Date of Death	(B) Age at Death
Feb. 27, 1845	52	Nov. 28, 1872	Retirement	27	80	Dec. 13, 1873	81
Sept. 23, 1845	55	Sept. 4, 1851	Death	5	61	Sept. 4, 1851	61
Aug. 10, 1846	52	Jan. 31, 1870	Retirement	23	75	Sept. 25, 1870	76
Oct. 10, 1851	41	Sept. 30, 1857	Resignation	5	47	Sept. 15, 1874	64
Apr. 11, 1853	41	Apr. 30, 1861	Resignation	8	49	Mar. 12, 1889	77
Jan. 21, 1858	54	July 25, 1881	Death	23	77	July 25, 1881	77
Jan. 27, 1862	57	Jan. 25, 1881	Retirement	18	76	June 8, 1884	79
July 21, 1862	46	Oct. 13, 1890	Death	28	74	Oct. 13, 1890	74
Dec. 10, 1862	47	Mar. 4, 1877	Resignation	14	61	June 26, 1886	71
May 20, 1863	46	Dec. 1, 1897	Retirement	34	81	Apr. 9, 1899	82
Mar. 14, 1870	61	Dec. 14, 1880	Retirement	10	72	Aug. 19, 1895	87
Mar. 23, 1870	57	Jan. 22, 1892	Death	21	78	Jan. 22, 1892	78
Jan. 9, 1873	62	Jan. 27, 1882	Disability	9	71	Mar. 24, 1886	75
Dec. 10, 1877	44	Oct. 14, 1911	Death	33	78	Oct. 14, 1911	78
Jan. 5, 1881	56	May 14, 1887	Death	6	62	May 14, 1887	62
May 17, 1881	56	Mar. 22, 1889	Death	7	64	Mar. 22, 1889	64
Jan. 9, 1882	53	Sept. 15, 1902	Death	20	74	Sept. 15, 1902	74
Apr. 3, 1882	62	July 7, 1893	Death	11	73	July 7, 1893	73
Jan. 18, 1888	62	Jan. 23, 1893	Death	5	67	Jan. 23, 1893	67
Jan. 6, 1890	52	Mar. 28, 1910	Death	20	72	Mar. 28, 1910	72
Jan. 5, 1891	54	May 28, 1906	Retirement	15	70	Sept. 4, 1913	77
Oct. 10, 1892	60	Feb. 23, 1903	Retirement	10	71	Aug. 2, 1924	92
Mar. 4, 1893	60	Aug. 8, 1895	Death	2	63	Aug. 8, 1895	63
Mar. 12, 1894	48	Dec. 18, 1910	Promotion	16	65	May 19, 1921	75

ASSOCIATE JUSTICES	Place of Birth	Date of Birth	State Appointed From	Appointed by President
Rufus W. Peckham	New York	Nov. 8, 1838	New York	Cleveland
Joseph McKenna	Pennsylvania	Aug. 10, 1843	California	McKinley
Oliver Wendell Holmes, Jr.	Massachusetts	Mar. 8, 1841	Massachusetts	Roosevelt, T.
William R. Day	Ohio	Apr. 17, 1849	Ohio	Roosevelt, T.
William H. Moody	Massachusetts	Dec. 23, 1853	Massachusetts	Roosevelt, T.
Horace H. Lurton	Kentucky	Feb. 26, 1844	Tennessee	Taft
Charles Evans Hughes	New York	Apr. 11, 1862	New York	Taft
Willis Van Devanter	Indiana	Apr. 17, 1859	Wyoming	Taft
Joseph Rucker Lamar	Georgia	Oct. 14, 1857	Georgia	Taft
Mahlon Pitney	New Jersey	Feb. 5, 1858	New Jersey	Taft
James Clark McReynolds	Kentucky	Feb. 3, 1862	Tennessee	Wilson
Louis D. Brandeis	Kentucky	Nov. 13, 1856	Massachusetts	Wilson
John H. Clarke	Ohio	Sept. 18, 1857	Ohio	Wilson
George Sutherland	England	Mar. 25, 1862	Utah	Harding
Pierce Butler	Minnesota	Mar. 17, 1866	Minnesota	Harding
Edward T. Sanford	Tennessee	July 23, 1865	Tennessee	Harding
Harlan Fiske Stone	New Hampshire	Oct. 11, 1872	New York	Coolidge
Owen J. Roberts	Pennsylvania	May 2, 1875	Pennsylvania	Hoover
Benjamin Nathan Cardozo	New York	May 24, 1870	New York	Hoover
Hugo L. Black	Alabama	Feb. 27, 1886	Alabama	Roosevelt, F.
Stanley F. Reed	Kentucky	Dec. 31, 1884	Kentucky	Roosevelt, F.
Felix Frankfurter	Austria	Nov. 15, 1882	Massachusetts	Roosevelt, F.
William O. Douglas	Minnesota	Oct. 16, 1898	Connecticut	Roosevelt, F.
Frank W. Murphy	Michigan	Apr. 13, 1890	Michigan	Roosevelt, F.

(A) Judicial Oath Taken	(B) Age Oath Taken	Date Service Terminated	Service Terminated By	(B) Years of Service	(B) Age at End of Term	Date of Death	(B) Age at Death
Jan. 6, 1896	57	Oct. 24, 1909	Death	13	70	Oct. 24, 1909	70
Jan. 26, 1898	54	Jan. 5, 1925	Retirement	26	81	Nov. 21, 1926	83
Dec. 8, 1902	61	Jan. 12, 1932	Retirement	29	90	Mar. 6, 1935	93
Mar. 2, 1903	53	Nov. 13, 1922	Retirement	19	73	July 9, 1923	74
Dec. 17, 1906	52	Nov. 20, 1910	Disability	3	56	July 2, 1917	63
Jan. 3, 1910	65	July 12, 1914	Death	4	70	July 12, 1914	70
Oct. 10, 1910	48	June 10, 1916	Resignation	5	54	Aug. 27, 1948	86
Jan. 3, 1911	51	June 2, 1937	Retirement	26	78	Feb. 8, 1941	81
Jan. 3, 1911	53	Jan. 2, 1916	Death	4	58	Jan. 2, 1916	58
Mar. 18, 1912	54	Dec. 31, 1922	Disability	10	64	Dec. 9, 1924	66
Oct. 12, 1914	52	Jan. 31, 1941	Retirement	26	78	Aug. 24, 1946	84
June 5, 1916	59	Feb. 13, 1939	Retirement	22	82	Oct. 5, 1941	84
Oct. 9, 1916	59	Sept. 18, 1922	Resignation	5	65	Mar. 22, 1945	87
Oct. 2, 1922	60	Jan. 17, 1938	Retirement	15	75	July 18, 1942	80
Jan. 2, 1923	56	Nov. 16, 1939	Death	16	73	Nov. 16, 1939	73
Feb. 19, 1923	57	Mar. 8, 1930	Death	7	64	Mar. 8, 1930	64
Mar. 2, 1925	52	July 2, 1941	Promotion	16	68	Apr. 22, 1946	73
June 2, 1930	55	July 31, 1945	Resignation	15	70	May 17, 1955	80
Mar. 14, 1932	61	July 9, 1938	Death	6	68	July 9, 1938	68
Aug. 19, 1937	51	Sept. 17, 1971	Retirement	34	85	Sept. 25, 1971	85
Jan. 31, 1938	53	Feb. 25, 1957	Retirement	19	72	Apr. 2, 1980	95
Jan. 30, 1939	56	Aug. 28, 1962	Retirement	23	79	Feb. 22, 1965	82
Apr. 17, 1939	40	Nov. 12, 1975	Retirement	36	77	Jan. 19, 1980	81
Feb. 5, 1940	49	July 19, 1949	Death	9	59	July 19, 1949	59

ASSOCIATE JUSTICES	Place of Birth	Date of Birth	State Appointed From	Appointed by President
James F. Byrnes	S. Carolina	May 2, 1879	S. Carolina	Roosevelt, F.
Robert H. Jackson	Pennsylvania	Feb. 13, 1892	New York	Roosevelt, F.
Wiley B. Rutledge	Kentucky	July 20, 1894	Iowa	Roosevelt, F.
Harold H. Burton	Massachusetts	June 22, 1888	Ohio	Truman
Tom C. Clark	Texas	Sept. 23, 1899	Texas	Truman
Sherman Minton	Indiana	Oct. 20, 1890	Indiana	Truman
John Marshall Harlan (II)	Illinois	May 20, 1899	New York	Eisenhower
William J. Brennan, Jr.	New Jersey	Apr. 25, 1906	New Jersey	Eisenhower
Charles E. Whittaker	Kansas	Feb. 22, 1901	Missouri	Eisenhower
Potter Stewart	Michigan	Jan. 23, 1915	Ohio	Eisenhower
Byron R. White	Colorado	June 8, 1917	Colorado	Kennedy
Arthur J. Goldberg	Illinois	Aug. 8, 1908	Illinois	Kennedy
Abe Fortas	Tennessee	June 19, 1910	Tennessee	Johnson, L.
Thurgood Marshall	Maryland	July 2, 1908	New York	Johnson, L.
Harry A. Blackmun	Illinois	Nov. 12, 1908	Minnesota	Nixon
Lewis F. Powell, Jr.	Virginia	Sept. 19, 1907	Virginia	Nixon
William H. Rehnquist	Wisconsin	Oct. 1, 1924	Arizona	Nixon
John Paul Stevens	Illinois	Apr. 20, 1920	Illinois	Ford
Sandra Day O'Connor	Texas	Mar. 26, 1930	Arizona	Reagan
Antonin Scalia	New Jersey	Mar. 11, 1936	Virginia	Reagan
Anthony M. Kennedy	California	July 23, 1936	California	Reagan
David H. Souter	Massachusetts	Sept. 17, 1939	New Hampshire	Bush
Clarence Thomas	Georgia	June 23, 1948	Georgia	Bush

(A) Judicial Oath Taken	(B) Age Oath Taken	Date Service Terminated	Service Terminated By	(B) Years of Service	(B) Age at End of Term	Date of Death	(B) Age at Death
July 8, 1941	62	Oct. 3, 1942	Resignation	1	63	Apr. 9, 1972	92
July 11, 1941	49	Oct. 9, 1954	Death	13	62	Oct. 9, 1954	62
Feb. 15, 1943	48	Sept. 10, 1949	Death	6	55	Sept. 10, 1949	55
Oct. 1, 1945	57	Oct. 13, 1958	Retirement	13	70	Oct. 28, 1964	76
Aug. 24, 1949	49	June 12, 1967	Retirement	17	67	June 13, 1977	77
Oct. 12, 1949	58	Oct. 15, 1956	Retirement	7	65	Apr. 9, 1965	74
Mar. 28, 1955	55	Sept. 23, 1971	Retirement	16	72	Dec. 29, 1971	72
Oct. 16, 1956	50	July 20, 1990	Retirement	33	84		
Mar. 25, 1957	56	Mar. 31, 1962	Disability	5	61	Nov. 26, 1973	72
Oct. 14, 1958	43	July 3, 1981	Retirement	23	66	Dec. 7, 1985	70
Apr. 16, 1962	44						
Oct. 1, 1962	54	July 25, 1965	Resignation	2	56	Jan. 19, 1990	81
Oct. 4, 1965	55	May 14, 1969	Resignation	3	58	Apr. 5, 1982	71
Oct. 2, 1967	59	June 17, 1991	Retirement	23	82		
June 9, 1970	61						
Jan. 7, 1972	64	June 26, 1987	Retirement	15	79		
Jan. 7, 1972	47	Sept. 26, 1986	Promotion	14	61		
Dec. 19, 1975	55						
Sept. 25, 1981	51						
Sept. 26, 1986	50						
Feb. 18, 1988	51						
Oct. 9, 1990	51						
Oct. 23, 1991	43						

(A) The date a Member of the Court took his judicial oath is here used as the date of the beginning of his service, for until that oath is taken he is not vested with the prerogatives of his office. Individuals who did not complete the necessary steps toward becoming a Member are not carried on this list.

(B) All calculations regarding ages or years of service are based on the age or service of the individual on his latest anniversary. Example: Chief Justice Rutledge actually served from August 12, 1795, to December 15, 1795, and is here carried as "0" years of service; and Mr. Justice Blair, who served from February 2, 1790, to January 27, 1796 — 5 years, 11 months, and 25 days — is carried as 5 years.

(C) Five Chief Justices served as Associate Justices. They are counted once in the total number of Justices.

The information in this chart was provided by the Curator's Office of the United States Supreme Court.

TABLE OF SUCCESSION OF THE JUSTICES OF THE SUPREME COURT

Judiciary Act of 1789 Provided for a Chief Justice and Five Associate Justices

Year	Chief Justice	Seat 2	Seat 3	Seat 4	Seat 5	Seat 6	Year
1789	John Jay NY CJ 1789–1795	John Rutledge* SC 1790–1791	William Cushing MA 1790–1810	James Iredell NC 1790–1799	James Wilson PA 1789–1798	John Blair, Jr. VA 1790–1796	1789
1790	John Rutledge* SC CJ 1795 Oliver Ellsworth CT CJ 1795–1800	Thomas Johnson MD 1792–1793 William Paterson NJ 1793–1806					1790
1800	John Marshall VA CJ 1801–1835	H. Brockholst Livingston NY 1807–1823		Alfred Moore NC 1800–1804 William Johnson SC 1804–1834	Bushrod Washington VA 1799–1829	Samuel Chase MD 1796–1811	1800
1810			Joseph Story MA 1812–1845			Gabriel Duvall MD 1811–1835	1810
1820		Smith Thompson NY 1823–1843					1820
1830	Roger Brooke Taney MD CJ 1836–1864			James M. Wayne GA 1835–1867	Henry Baldwin PA 1830–1844	Philip P. Barbour VA 1836–1841	1830
1840		Samuel Nelson NY 1845–1872	Levi Woodbury NH 1845–1851	NO NEW APPOINTMENT	Robert C. Grier PA 1846–1870	Peter V. Daniel VA 1842–1860	1840
1850			Benjamin R. Curtis MA 1851–1857 Nathan Clifford ME 1858–1881				1850
1860	Salmon Portland Chase OH CJ 1864–1873					Samuel F. Miller IA 1862–1890	1860
1870	Morrison R. Waite OH CJ 1874–1888	Ward Hunt NY 1873–1882			William Strong PA 1870–1880		1870
1880	Melville Weston Fuller IL CJ 1888–1910	Samuel Blatchford NY 1882–1893	Horace Gray MA 1882–1902		William B. Woods GA 1881–1887 Lucius Q. C. Lamar MS 1888–1893		1880
1890							1890

*Served as both Associate Justice and Chief Justice

Seat created 1807	Seats created 1837		Seat created 1863	Seat created 1869

1789					1789
1790					1790
1800					1800
	Thomas Todd KY 1807–1826				
1810					1810
1820					1820
	Robert Trimble KY 1826–1828				
1830	John McLean OH 1830–1861				1830
		John Catron TN 1837–1865	John McKinley AL 1838–1852		
1840					1840
		NO NEW APPOINTMENT			
1850					1850
			John A. Campbell AL 1853–1861		
1860	Noah H. Swayne OH 1862–1881		David Davis IL 1862–1877	Stephen J. Field CA 1863–1897	1860
1870				Joseph P. Bradley NJ 1870–1892	1870
			John Marshall Harlan KY 1877–1911		
1880	Stanley Matthews OH 1881 1889				1880
1890					1890

Judiciary Act of 1789 Provided for a Chief Justice and Five Associate Justices

1890		Edward D. White* LA 1894–1910		Howell E. Jackson TN 1893–1895 Rufus W. Peckham NY 1896–1909	Henry B. Brown MI 1891–1906
1900			Oliver Wendell Holmes, Jr. MA 1902–1932		William H. Moody MA 1906–1910
1910	Edward D. White* LA CJ 1910–1921	Willis Van Devanter WY 1911–1937		Horace H. Lurton TN 1910–1914 James Clark McReynolds TN 1914–1941	Joseph Rucker Lamar GA 1911–1916 Louis D. Brandeis MA 1916–1939
1920	William Howard Taft CT CJ 1921–1930				
1930	Charles Evans Hughes* NY CJ 1930–1941	Hugo L. Black AL 1937–1971	Benjamin Nathan Cardozo NY 1932–1938 Felix Frankfurter MA 1939–1962		William O. Douglas CT 1939–1975
1940	Harlan Fiske Stone* NY CJ 1941–46 Fred M. Vinson KY CJ 1946–1953			James F. Byrnes SC 1941–1942 Wiley B. Rutledge IA 1943–1949 Sherman Minton IN 1949–1956	
1950	Earl Warren CA CJ 1953–1969			William J. Brennan, Jr. NJ 1956–1990	
1960			Arthur J. Goldberg IL 1962–1965 Abe Fortas TN 1965–1969 Harry A. Blackmun MN 1970–		
1970	Warren E. Burger VA CJ 1969–1986	Lewis F. Powell, Jr. VA 1972–1987			John Paul Stevens IL 1975–
1980	William H. Rehnquist* VA CJ 1986–	Anthony M. Kennedy CA 1988–			
1990				David H. Souter NH 1990–	

*Served as both Associate Justice and Chief Justice

Seat Created 1807	Seats Created 1837		Seat Created 1863	Seat Created 1869
1890 David J. Brewer KS 1890–1910				George Shiras, Jr. PA 1892–1903 **1890**
			Joseph McKenna CA 1898–1925	
1900				William R. Day OH 1903 1922 **1900**
1910 Charles Evans Hughes* NY 1910–1916 John H. Clarke OH 1916–1922		Mahlon Pitney NJ 1912–1922		**1910**
1920 George Sutherland UT 1922–1938		Edward T. Sanford TN 1923–1930	Harlan Fiske Stone* NY 1925–1941	Pierce Butler MN 1923–1939 **1920**
1930		Owen J. Roberts PA 1930–1945		**1930**
Stanley F. Reed KY 1938–1957				
1940		Harold H. Burton OH 1945 1958	Robert H. Jackson NY 1941–1954	Frank W. Murphy MI 1940–1949 **1940** Tom C. Clark TX 1949–1967
1950				**1950**
Charles E. Whittaker MO 1957–1962		Potter Stewart OH 1958–1981	John Marshall Harlan (II) NY 1955–1971	
1960 Byron R. White CO 1962–				Thurgood Marshall NY 1967–1991 **1960**
1970			William H. Rehnquist* AZ 1972–1986	**1970**
1980		Sandra Day O'Connor AZ 1981–	Antonin Scalia VA 1986–	**1980**
1990				Clarence Thomas GA 1991– **1990**

The information in this chart was provided by the Curator's Office of the United States Supreme Court.

281

Bibliography

THE COURT

American Bar Association. "The Supreme Court—Its Homes Past and Present." 27 *ABA Journal* (1941).

Barkan, S. M., comp. *The Supreme Court in American History: A Selected Bibliography of Books Published After 1977.* Washington, D.C.: Library of the Supreme Court of the United States, 1981.

Blaustein, A. P., and R. M. Merkey. *The First One Hundred Justices: Statistical Studies on the Supreme Court of the United States.* Hamden, Conn.: Archon Books, the Shoestring Press, Inc., 1978.

Carson, H. L. *The History of the Supreme Court of the United States with Biographies of All the Chief and Associate Justices.* Philadelphia: P. W. Ziegler Co., 1902.

Corwin, E. S. *The Constitution and What It Means Today.* 14th ed. Princeton, N. J.: Princeton University Press, 1978.

Elliott, S. P., gen. ed. *Reference Guide to the U.S. Supreme Court.* New York: Facts on File Publications, Inc. (Sachem Publications Associates Inc.), 1986.

Frankfurter, F., and J. M. Landis. *The Business of the Supreme Court: A Study in the Federal Judicial System.* New York: The Macmillan Company, 1927.

Freund, P. A. *The Supreme Court of the United States: Its Business, Purposes, and Performance.* Cleveland: Meridian Books, World Publishing Co., 1961.

Freund, P. A., gen. ed. *History of the Supreme Court of the United States.* New York: Macmillan Publishing Co., Inc., 1974.

Friedman, L., and F. L. Israel, eds. *The Justices of the United States Supreme Court, 1789-1978, Their Lives and Major Opinions.* Vols. 1-5. New York: Chelsea House, 1980. [Updated volume due in 1993.]

Harrell, M. A. *Equal Justice Under Law: The Supreme Court in American Life.* Washington, D.C.: The Foundation of the American Bar Association with the cooperation of the National Geographic Society, 1975.

Hughes, C. E. *The Supreme Court of the United States: Its Foundation, Methods, and Achievements: An Interpretation.* New York: Columbia University Press, 1928.

Madison, J., A. Hamilton, and J. Jay. *The Federalist Papers.* Introduction by C. Rossiter. New York: The New American Library, Mentor Books, 1961.

Martin, F. S., and R. U. Goehlert. *The Supreme Court—A Bibliography.* Washington, D.C.: Congressional Quarterly, Inc., 1990.

McCloskey, R. *The American Supreme Court.* Chicago: The University of Chicago Press, 1960.

Peltason, J. W. *Understanding the Constitution.* 4th ed. New York: Holt Rinehart and Winston, 1959.

Pollack, L. H., ed. *The Constitution and the Supreme Court: A Documentary History.* Cleveland and New York: The World Publishing Co., 1966.

Shnayerson, R. *The Illustrated History of the Supreme Court of the United States.* New York: Harry N. Abrams, Inc., in association with the Supreme Court Historical Society, 1986.

Stephenson, D. G., Jr. *The Supreme Court and the American Republic—An Annotated Bibliography.* New York: Garland Publishing, Inc., 1981.

Swindler, W. F., ed. *Supreme Court Historical Society Yearbook.* Washington, D. C.: Supreme Court Historical Society, 1975.

Swisher, C. B. *American Constitutional Development.* 2d ed. Cambridge: Houghlin Mifflin Co., The Riverside Press, 1954.

Warren, C. *The Supreme Court in United States History.* 2 vols., rev. ed. Boston: Little, Brown and Co., 1937.

Witt, E., ed. *Guide to the United States Supreme Court.* Washington, D. C.: Congressional Quarterly, Inc., 1990.

THE JUSTICES

BALDWIN, HENRY

Baldwin, H. *A General View of the Origin and Nature of the United States.* Philadelphia: Lippincott, 1837.

Taylor, F. M. "The Political and Civil Career of Henry Baldwin, 1799–1830." 24 *Western Pennsylvania Historical Magazine* 37 (1941).

BARBOUR, PHILIP P.

Baldwin H. *A General View of the Origin and Nature of the Constitution and Government of the United States.* Philadelphia: J. C. Clark, 1837.

Cynn, P. P. "Philip Pendleton Barbour." 4 *John P. Branch Historical Papers of Randolph-Macon College* 67 (1913).

BLACK, HUGO L.

Ball, H. *The Vision and the Dream of Justice Hugo L. Black: An Examination of a Judicial Philosophy.* University, Ala.: University of Alabama Press, 1975.

Black, H. L. *A Constitutional Faith.* New York: Knopf, 1968.

Black, H. L. *One Man's Stand for Freedom: Mr. Justice Black and the Bill of Rights: A Collection of His Supreme Court Decisions.* Selected and edited with an introduction and notes by I. Dilliard. New York: Knopf, 1963.

Black, H. L., Jr. *My Father: A Remembrance.* New York: Random House, 1975.

Davis, H. B. *Uncle Hugo: An Intimate Portrait of Mr. Justice Black.* Amarillo, Texas: privately published, 1965.

Dunne, G. T. *Hugo Black and the Judicial Revolution.* New York: Simon & Schuster, 1977.

Hamilton, V. V. *Hugo Black: The Alabama Years.* Baton Rouge: Louisiana State University Press, 1972.

Hamilton, V. V., ed. *Hugo Black and the Bill of Rights.* University, Ala.: University of Alabama Press, 1978.

Mendelson, W. *Justices Black and Frankfurter: Conflict in the Court.* 2d ed. Chicago: University of Chicago Press, 1966.

Strickland, S. P., ed. *Hugo Black and the Supreme Court: A Symposium.* Indianapolis: Bobbs-Merrill, 1967.

United States Congress, Joint Committee on Printing. *Hugo Lafayette Black, 1886–1971: Memorial Addresses and Tributes.* Washington, D.C.: U.S. Government Printing Office, 1972.

Williams, C. *Hugo L. Black: A Study in the Judicial Process.* Baltimore: Johns Hopkins University Press, 1950.

BLACKMUN, HARRY A.

Blackmun, Harry A. "Movement and Countermovement." 338 *Drake Law Review* 4 (1988–89).

Blackmun, Harry A. "Section 1983 and Federal Protection of Individual Rights—Will the Statute Remain Alive or Fade Away?" 60 *New York University Law Review* 1 (1985).

BLAIR, JOHN, JR.

Drinard, J. E. "John Blair, Jr." 39 *Proceedings of Virginia State Bar Association* 436 (1927).

Horner, F. *History of the Blair, Banister and Braxton Families.* Philadelphia: 1898.

BLATCHFORD, SAMUEL

Blatchford, S. *Reports of Cases in Prize, Argued and Determined in the Circuit and District Courts of the United States for the Southern District of New York, 1861–1865.* New York: Baker, Voorhis, 1866.

Shiras III, G. *Justice George Shiras, Jr., of Pittsburgh: A Chronicle of His Family, Life, and Times.* Edited and completed by W. Shiras. Pittsburgh: University of Pittsburgh Press, 1953.

BRADLEY, JOSEPH P.

Bradley, J. P. *Family Notes Respecting the Bradley Family of Fairchild.* Newark, N.J.: privately published, 1894.

Bradley, J. P. *Miscellaneous Writing of Hon. Joseph P. Bradley; A Review of His Judicial Record by William Draper Lewis; An Account of His Dissenting Opinions by A. Q. Keasbey.* Edited and compiled by his son C. Bradley. Newark, N.J.: L. J. Harham, 1902.

Fairman, C. "The Education of A Justice: Justice Bradley and Some of His Colleagues." 1 *Stanford Law Review* 2 (January 1949), pp. 217–255.

Fairman, C. "Mr. Justice Bradley." In A. Dunham and P. B. Knowland, *Mr. Justice.* Chicago: University of Chicago Press, 1964.

BRANDEIS, LOUIS D.

Baker, L. *Brandeis and Frankfurter: A Dual Biography.* New York: Harper & Row, 1984.

Bickel, A. M. *The Unpublished Opinions of Mr. Justice Brandeis: The Supreme Court at Work.* Cambridge: Harvard University Press, 1957; Chicago: Chicago University Press, Phoenix Books, 1967.

Brandeis, L. D. "Half Brother, Half Son." *The Letters of Louis D. Brandeis to Felix Frankfurter,* edited by M. I. Urofsky and D. W. Levy. Norman: University of Oklahoma Press, 1991.

Frankfurter, F. *Mr. Justice Brandeis.* New Haven: Yale University Press, 1932; New York: Da Capo Press, 1972.

Freund, P. A. *The Writings of Louis D. Brandeis.* Indianapolis: Bobbs-Merrill, 1966.

Gal, A. *Brandeis of Boston.* Cambridge: Harvard University Press, 1980.

Konefsky, S. J. *The Legacy of Holmes and Brandeis: A Study in the Influence of Ideas.* New York: Macmillan, 1956; New York: Da Capo Press, 1974.

Lief, A., ed. *Brandeis: The Personal History of an American Ideal.* New York: Stackpole & Sons, 1936.

Mason, A. T. *Brandeis, A Free Man's Life.* New York: Viking, 1946.

Mersky, R. M. *Louis Dembitz Brandeis, 1856–1941: A Bibliography.* Yale Law Library Publications, No. 15, April 1958; Littleton, Colo.: F. B. Rothman, 1987.

Noble, I. *Firebrand for Justice: A Biography of Louis Dembitz Brandeis.* Philadelphia: Westminster, 1969.

Paper, L. J. *Brandeis: An Intimate Biography of America's Truly Great Supreme Court Justice.* Englewood Cliffs, N.J.: Prentice Hall, 1983.

Pollack, E. H., ed. *The Brandeis Reader.* Dobbs Ferry, N.Y.: Oceana Publications, 1956.

Strum, P. *Louis D. Brandeis: Justice for the People.* Cambridge: Harvard University Press, 1984.

Todd, A. L. *Justice on Trial: The Case of Louis D. Brandeis.* New York: McGraw-Hill, 1964.

BRENNAN, WILLIAM J., JR.

" A Tribute to Justice William J. Brennan, Jr." 104 *Harvard Law Review* 1 (1990).

Brennan, W. J. *An Affair with Freedom.* Edited by S. J. Friedman. New York: Atheneum, 1967.

"The Reporter Honors Justice William J. Brennan, Jr." 6 *The Reporter* 1 (Spring 1984), pp. 8–50.

Robins, W. M. "A Bibliography of Associate Justice William J. Brennan, Jr." 12 *Seton Hall Law Review* 2 (1982), pp. 430–444.

"Special Issue Dedicated to Justice William Brennan." 20 *John Marshall Law Review* 1 (Fall 1986), pp. 1–199.

"Tributes." 100 *Yale Law Journal* 1113 (1991).

BREWER, DAVID J.

Butler, H. H. "Memorial Note: Melville Weston Fuller, David Josiah Brewer." *American Journal of International Law* (October 1910), pp. 909–921.

Lardner, L. A. *The Constitutional Doctrines of Justice David Josiah Brewer.* Thesis: Princeton University, 1938. Ann Arbor, Mich.: University Microfilms International, 1981.

Stanley, E. D. "David J. Brewer, 1837–1910; A Kansan on the United States Supreme Court." Thesis: Graduate Division, Kansas State Teachers College, Emporia, 1964.

BROWN, HENRY B.

Butler, C. H. "Mr. Justice Brown." 18 *Green Bag* 6 (June 1906).

Kent, C. A. *Memoir of Henry Billings Brown.* New York: Dunfield, 1915.

Paul, A. M. *Conservative Crisis and the Rule of Law.* Ithaca, N.Y.: Cornell University Press, 1960.

Warner, R. M. "Detroit's First Supreme Court Justice." 13 *Detroit Historical Society Bulletin* (May 1957), pp. 8–13.

BURGER, WARREN E.

Anderson, B., ed. *Delivery of Justice.* Minneapolis: West Publishing Co., 1990.

Blasi, V. "Mr. Chief Justice Burger on the State of the Judiciary." 15 *Suffolk University Law Review* 5 (December 1981), pp. 1105–1124.

Blasi, V., ed. *The Burger Court: The Counter-Revolution That Wasn't*. New Haven: Yale University Press, 1983.

Lee, F. G. *Neither Conservative Nor Liberal: The Burger Court on Civil Rights and Civil Liberties*. Melbourne, Fla.: Krieger Publishing, 1983.

Mason, A. T. "The Burger Court in Historical Perspective." 47 *New York State Bar Journal* 2 (February 1975), pp. 87–91, 122–132.

Newell, D. "Chief Justice Burger and the English Experience: Suggested Reforms of American Legal Education." 53 *Notre Dame Lawyer* 5 (June 1978), pp. 934–940.

Pfeffer, L. *Religion, State and the Burger Court*. Buffalo, N.Y.: Prometheus Books, 1984.

Schwartz, B. *The Ascent of Pragmatism: The Burger Court in Action*. Reading, Mass.: Addison-Wesley Pub. Co., 1990.

BURTON, HAROLD H.

Berry, M. F. *Stability, Security, and Continuity: Mr. Justice Burton and Decisionmaking in the Supreme Court, 1945–1958*. Westport, Conn.: Greenwood Press, 1978.

Hudson, E. G., ed. *The Occasional Papers of Mr. Justice Burton*. Brunswick, Maine: Bowdoin College, 1969.

Marquardt, R. G. "The Judicial Justice: Mr. Justice Burton and the Supreme Court." Thesis: University of Wisconsin, 1973.

Provine, D. M. *Case Selection in the United States Supreme Court*. Chicago: University of Chicago Press, 1980.

BUTLER, PIERCE

Brown, F. J. *The Social and Economic Philosophy of Pierce Butler*. Washington, D.C.: Catholic University, 1945.

Danelski, D. J. *A Supreme Court Justice Is Appointed*. New York: Random House, 1964.

Kearney, E. N. *Four Economic Conservatives and Civil Liberties: A Study of the Positions of Justices Butler, McReynolds, Sutherland and Van Devanter, with Emphasis on the Period 1823–1937*. Thesis: The American University. Ann Arbor, Mich.: University Microfilms International, 1982.

BYRNES, JAMES F.

Byrnes, J. F. *All in One Lifetime*. New York: Harper, 1958.

Hogan, F. J. "Associate Justice James F. Byrnes." 27 *American Bar Association Journal* (August 1941), pp. 475–478.

"In Memoriam, Honorable James Francis Byrnes." Proceedings before the Supreme Court of the United States. Washington, D.C.: United States Supreme Court (1972).

Petit, W. "Justice Byrnes and the Supreme Court." 6 *South Carolina Law Quarterly* 423 (1954).

CAMPBELL, JOHN A.

Connor, H. G. *John Archibald Campbell, Associate Judge of the United States Supreme Court, 1853–1861*. Boston and New York: Houghton Mifflin, 1920.

Holt, J., Jr. "The Resignation of Mr. Justice Campbell." 12 *Alabama Law Review* 105 (1959).

Jordan, C. "Last of the Jacksonians (Justice John Campbell)." *Supreme Court Historical Society Yearbook 1980*. Washington, D.C.

Mann, J. S. *The Political and Constitutional Thought of John Archibald Campbell*. Thesis: University of Alabama, 1966. Ann Arbor, Mich.: University Microfilms International, 1983.

CARDOZO, BENJAMIN NATHAN

Cardozo, B. N. *The Growth of the Law*. New Haven: Yale University Press, 1924.

Cardozo, B. N. *Law and Literature and Other Essays*. New York: Harcourt, Brace, 1931.

Cardozo, B. N. *The Nature of the Judicial Process*. New Haven: Yale University Press, 1921.

Cardozo, B. N. *Paradoxes of the Legal Science*. New York: Columbia University Press, 1928.

Hall, M. E., ed. *Selected Writing of B. N. Cardozo*. New York: Fallon, 1947.

Hellman, G. S. *Benjamin N. Cardozo: American Judge*. New York: Whittlesey, 1940.

Levy, B. H. *Cardozo and the Frontiers of Legal Thinking: With Selected Opinions*. 2nd ed. Cleveland: Case-Western Reserve University, 1970.

Pollard, J. P. *Mr. Justice Cardozo: A Liberal Mind in Action*. New York: Yorktown Press, 1935.

CATRON, JOHN

Chandler, W. "The Centenary of Associate Justice John Catron of the United States Supreme Court." Address by W. Chandler at the 56th annual session of the Bar Association of Tennessee, Memphis, June 11, 1937. Washington, D.C.: Government Printing Office, 1937.

Gass, E. C. "The Constitutional Opinions of Justice John Catron." 8 *East Tennessee Historical Society's Publications* 54 (1936).

Foote, H. S. "Judge Catron." In *The Bench and Bar of the South and Southwest*, by H. S. Foote, 1876. St. Louis: Soule, Thomas & Wentworth, 1876.

CHASE, SALMON PORTLAND

Chase, S. P. *Diaries and Correspondence*. Reprint. New York: Da Capo Press, 1971.

Hart, A. B. *Salmon Portland Chase*. Boston: Houghton Mifflin, 1899.

Johnson, B. T. *Reports on Cases Decided by Chief Justice Chase in the Circuit Court of the United States for the Fourth Circuit*. Reprint. New York: Da Capo Press, 1972.

Schuckers, J. W. *The Life and Public Services of Salmon Portland Chase*. Reprint of the 1874 edition. New York: Da Capo Press, 1970.

CHASE, SAMUEL

Elsmere, J. S. *Justice Samuel Chase*. Muncie, Ind.: Janevar Pub. Co., 1980.

Haw, J. "Stormy Patriot: The Life of Samuel Chase." Baltimore: Maryland Historical Society, 1980.

United States Senate. *Trial of Samuel Chase, an Associate Justice of the Supreme Court Impeached by the House of Representatives for High Crimes and Misdemeanors Before the Senate of the United States*. 8th Congress, 2d session, 1805.

CLARK, TOM C.

Dorin, D. D. "Justice Tom Clark and the Right of Defendants in State Courts." Thesis: University of Virginia, 1974.

Dutton, C. B. "Mr. Justice Tom Clark." 26 *Indiana Law Journal* 169 (1951).

Kirkendall, R. J. *The Truman Period as a Research Field*. New York: Columbia University Press, 1967.

"A Symposium on the Tom C. Clark Papers." Austin: Tarleton Law Library Publications, 1987.

CLARKE, JOHN H.

Levitan, D. M. "The Jurisprudence of Mr. Justice Clarke." 7 *Miami Law Quarterly* 44 (1952).

Warner, H. L. *The Life of Mr. Justice Clarke: A Testimony to the Power of Liberal Dissent in America*. Cleveland: Western Reserve University, 1959.

Wittke, C. F. "Mr. Justice Clarke: A Supreme Court Judge in Retirement." 36 *Mississippi Valley Historical Review* 1 (June 1949).

CLIFFORD, NATHAN

Clifford, P. G. *Nathan Clifford, Democrat (1803–1881)*. New York, London: Putnam's Sons, 1922.

CURTIS, BENJAMIN R.

Curtis, B. R., Jr. *A Memoir of Benjamin Robbins Curtis, L.L.D.* Boston: Little, Brown, 1897.

Leach, R. H. "Benjamin R. Curtis: Case Study of a Supreme Court Justice." Thesis: Princeton University, 1951.

Leach, R. H. "Benjamin Robbins Curtis: Judicial Misfit." 25 *New England Quarterly* (1952), pp. 507–523.

CUSHING, WILLIAM

Cushing, J. D. "The Cushing Court and the Abolition of Slavery in Massachusetts." 5 *American Journal of Legal History* 118 (1961).

Cushing, J. D. "A Revolutionary Conservative: The Public Life of William Cushing, 1732–1810." Thesis: Clark University, 1960.

Flanders, H. *The Lives and Times of the Chief Justices of the Supreme Court of the United States*. Vol. 2, *William Cushing*. [Reprint of the 1881 edition] Buffalo: W. S. Hein, 1972.

O'Brien, F. W. "The Pre-Marshall Court and the Role of William Cushing." 43 *Massachusetts Law Quarterly* 1 (March 1958).

DANIEL, PETER V.

Brown, H. B. "The Dissenting Opinions of Mr. Justice Daniel." 21 *American Law Review* (1887) and 46 *American Law Review* (1912).

Frank, J. P. *Justice Daniel Dissenting: A Biography of Peter V. Daniel, 1784–1860.* Cambridge: Harvard University Press, 1964.

Hendricks, B. M. *Bulwark of the Republic: A Biography of the Constitution.* Boston: Little, Brown, 1957.

DAVIS, DAVID

Dent, T. "David Davis of Illinois: A Sketch." 53 *American Law Review* (1919).

Fairman, C. *Mr. Justice Miller and the Supreme Court, 1862–1890.* Cambridge: Harvard University Press, 1939.

King, W. L. *Lincoln's Manager: David Davis.* Cambridge: Harvard University Press, 1960.

Kutler, S. I. *Judicial Power and Reconstruction Politics.* Chicago: University of Chicago Press, 1968.

DAY, WILLIAM R.

Day, W. R. "The Judicial Power of the Nation." 17 *Michigan Alumnus* 162 (March 1911).

McLean, J. E. *William Rufus Day: Supreme Court Justice from Ohio.* Baltimore: Johns Hopkins University Press, 1946.

DOUGLAS, WILLIAM O.

Ashmore, H. S., ed. *The William O. Douglas Inquiry into the State of Individual Freedom.* Boulder, Colo.: Westview, 1979.

Bosmajian, H. *Justice Douglas and Freedom of Speech.* Metuchen, N.J.: Scarecrow, 1980.

Countryman, V. *The Douglas Opinions.* New York: Random House, 1977.

Douglas, W. O. *The Court Years (1939–1975): The Autobiography of William O. Douglas.* New York: Random House, 1980.

Douglas, W. O. *Go East, Young Man; The Early Years. The Autobiography of William O. Douglas.* New York: Random House, 1974.

Douglas, W. O., ed. *Courts, Law and Judicial Process.* New York: Free Press, 1981.

Duram, J. C. *Justice William O. Douglas.* Boston: Twayne Publishers, 1981.

Simon, J. F. *Independent Journey: The Life of William O. Douglas.* New York: Harper & Row, 1980.

DUVALL, GABRIEL

Dilliard, I. "Gabriel Duvall." *Dictionary of American Biography,* Supplement I. New York: 1945.

ELLSWORTH, OLIVER

Brown, W. G. *The Life of Oliver Ellsworth.* New York: Macmillan, 1905; New York: Da Capo Press, 1970.

Jones, F. R. "Oliver Ellsworth" 13 *Green Bag* (November 1901).

Van Santvoord, G. *Sketches of the Lives, Times, and Judicial Services of the Chief Justices of the Supreme Court of the United States.* 2d ed. Edited by W. M. Scott. Buffalo: Hein, 1977.

Warren, C. "New Light on the History of the Federal Judiciary Act of 1789." 37 *Harvard Law Review* 1 (November 1923).

FIELD, STEPHEN J.

Field, S. J. *Personal Reminiscences of Early Days in California.* Washington, D.C.: privately published, 1893; New York: Da Capo Press, 1968.

Jones, W. C. "Justice Field's Opinions on Constitutional Law." 5 *California Law Review* 2 (January 1917).

Swisher, C. B. *Stephen J. Field: Craftsman of the Law.* Washington, D.C.: The Brookings Institution, 1930.

Turner, W. R. *Documents in Relation to the Charges Preferred by Stephen J. Field and Others.* San Francisco: privately published, 1853.

FORTAS, ABE

Fortas, A. *Concerning Dissent and Civil Disobedience.* New York: New American Library, 1968.

Heckart, R. J. *Justice Fortas and the First Amendment.* Thesis: State University of New York at Albany, 1973. Ann Arbor, Mich.: University Microfilms International, 1978.

Kalman, L. *Abe Fortas: A Biography.* New Haven: Yale University Press, 1990.

Shogan, R. *A Question of Judgment: The Fortas Case and the Struggle for the Supreme Court.* Indianapolis: Bobbs-Merrill, 1972.

FRANKFURTER, FELIX

Baker, L. *Brandeis and Frankfurter: A Dual Biography.* New York: Harper & Row, 1983.

Baker, L. *Felix Frankfurter.* New York: Coward, McCann, 1969.

Frankfurter, F. *Of Law and Men.* New York: Harcourt, Brace, 1956.

Frankfurter, F., and J. M. Landis. *The Business of the Supreme Court: A Study in the Federal Judicial System.* New York: The Macmillan Company, 1927.

Hirsch, H. N. *The Enigma of Felix Frankfurter.* New York: Basic Books, 1981.

Konefsky, S. J., ed. *The Constitutional World of Mr. Justice Frankfurter.* New York: Macmillan, 1949.

Kurland, P. B., ed. *Felix Frankfurter on the Supreme Court: Extrajudicial Essays on the Court and the Constitution.* Cambridge: Belknap Press of Harvard University Press, 1970.

Lash, J. P. *From the Diaries of Felix Frankfurter.* New York: Norton, 1975.

Parrish, M. E. *Felix Frankfurter and His Times: The Reform Years.* New York: Free Press, 1982.

Thomas, H. S., ed. *Felix Frankfurter, Scholar on the Bench.* Baltimore: Johns Hopkins Press, 1960.

FULLER, MELVILLE WESTON

Holmes, O. W. "Judge Putnam's Recollections of Melville Weston Fuller." 22 *Green Bag* (1910).

King, W. L. "Melville Weston Fuller: The 'Chief' and the Giants on the Court." 36 *American Bar Association Journal* (April 1950), pp. 293–296.

King, W. L. *Melville Weston Fuller: Chief Justice of the United States, 1888–1910.* New York: Macmillan, 1950; Chicago: University of Chicago Press, Phoenix Books, 1967.

Reeder, R. P. "Chief Justice Fuller." 59 *University of Pennsylvania Law Review and American Law Register* (1910/1911).

Wade, W. E. "Chief Justice Fuller, the Individualist on the Bench." 10 *Maine Law Review* 77 (1917).

GOLDBERG, ARTHUR J.

Bennett, R. W., W. H. Rehnquist, W. J. Brennan, et al. "In Memoriam: Arthur J. Goldberg, 1908–1990." 84 *Northwestern University Law Review* 3 and 4 (Spring/Summer 1990), pp. 807–831.

Goldberg, A. J. *The Defenses of Freedom: The Public Papers of Arthur J. Goldberg.* Edited by D. P. Moynihan. New York: Harper & Row, 1966.

Goldberg, A. J. *Equal Justice: The Supreme Court in the Warren Era.* Evanston, Ill.: Northwestern University Press, 1971.

Goldberg, A. J. *The Evolving Constitution: Essays on the Bill of Rights and the U.S. Supreme Court.* Edited with a foreword by N. Dorsen. Introduction by A. Cox. Middletown, Conn.: Wesleyan University Press, 1987.

"Remembrances of Justice Arthur J. Goldberg." 17 *Hastings Constitutional Law Quarterly* (Winter 1990), pp. 281–286.

Watts, T. J. "A Bibliography of Arthur J. Goldberg." 77 *Law Library Journal* 2 (1984–1985), pp. 307–338.

GRAY, HORACE

Hoar, G. F. "Memoir of Horace Gray." 18 *Proceedings of the Massachusetts Historical Society* (Second series, 1903–4/1905).

Mitchell, S. R. "Mr. Justice Horace Gray." Thesis: University of Wisconsin, 1961.

Spector, R. M. "Legal Historian on the United States Supreme Court: Justice Horace Gray, Jr., and the Historical Method." 12 *American Journal of Legal History* 3 (July 1968), pp. 181–210.

GRIER, ROBERT C.

Jones, F. R. "Robert Cooper Grier." 16 *Green Bag* 4 (1904), pp. 221–224.

HARLAN, JOHN MARSHALL

Clark, F. B. *The Constitutional Doctrine of Justice Harlan.* Series 33, No. 4. Baltimore: Johns Hopkins University Press, 1915; New York: Da Capo Press, 1969.

"John Marshall Harlan, 1833–1911." Symposium. *Kentucky Law Journal* (Spring 1958).

Latham, F. B. *The Great Dissenter: John Marshall Harlan.* New York: Cowles Book Co., 1970.

Porter, M. C. A. "John Marshall Harlan and the Laissez-Faire Courts." Thesis: University of Chicago, 1970.

Westin, A. F. "The First Justice Harlan: A Self-Portrait from His Private Papers." 46 *Kentucky Law Journal* 3 (Spring 1958), pp. 321–366.

HARLAN, JOHN MARSHALL (II)

Levin, M. "Justice Harlan: The Full Measure of the Man." 58 *American Bar Association Journal* 579 (1972).

"Mr. Justice John Marshall Harlan." Symposium. *Harvard Law Review* (December 1971).

Shapiro, D., ed. *The Evolution of a Judicial Philosophy: Selected Opinions and Papers of Justice John M. Harlan.* Cambridge: Harvard University Press, 1969.

HOLMES, OLIVER WENDELL, JR.

Biddle, F. *Mr. Justice Holmes.* New York: Scribner's, 1942.

Bowen, C. D. *A Yankee from Olympus: Justice Holmes and His Family.* Boston: Little Brown, 1944.

Burton, D. H., ed. *Oliver Wendell Holmes, Jr., What Manner of Liberal?* Melbourne, Fla.: Krieger Publishing, 1979.

Frankfurter, F. *Mr. Justice Holmes and the Supreme Court.* 2d ed. Cambridge, Mass.: Belknap Press of Harvard University Press, 1961.

Holmes, O. W. *Justice Holmes, Ex Cathedra.* Compiled and arranged by E. J. Bander. Charlottesville, Va.: Michie, 1966.

Holmes, O. W., Jr. *Collected Legal Papers.* New York: Harcourt, 1920.

Howe, M. de W. *Justice Oliver Wendell Holmes: The Proving Years, 1870–1882.* Cambridge: Harvard University Press, 1963.

Howe, M. de W. *Justice Oliver Wendell Holmes: The Shaping Years, 1841–1870.* Cambridge: Harvard University Press, 1957.

Hurst, W. J. *Justice Holmes and Legal History.* New York: Macmillan, 1964.

Konefsky, S. J. *The Legacy of Holmes and Brandeis: A Study in the Influence of Ideas.* New York: Macmillan, 1956; New York: Da Capo Press, 1974.

Lerner, M., ed. *The Mind and Faith of Justice Holmes.* Boston: Little, Brown, 1943.

Marke, J., ed. *The Holmes Reader.* 2d ed. Dobbs Ferry, N.Y.: Oceana Publications, 1964.

Shriver, H. C. *What Justice Holmes Wrote, and What Has Been Written About Him: A Bibliography, 1866–1976.* Compiled and edited with an introduction by H. C. Shriver. Potomac, Md.: Fox Hills Press, 1978.

HUGHES, CHARLES EVANS

Danelsik, D. J., and J. S. Tulchin, eds. *The Autobiographical Notes of Charles Evans Hughes.* Cambridge: Harvard University Press, 1973.

Hendel, S. *Charles Evans Hughes and the Supreme Court.* New York: Columbia University Press, 1951.

Hughes, C. E. *The Supreme Court of the United States: Its Foundation, Methods and Achievements, An Interpretation.* New York: Columbia University Press, 1966.

Kornberg, H. R. "Charles Evans Hughes in the Supreme Court: A Study in Judicial Philosophy and Voting Behavior." Thesis: Brown University, 1972.

Pusey, M. J. *Charles Evans Hughes.* New York: Macmillan, 1951.

Ransom, W. L. *Charles Evans Hughes: The Statesman as Shown in the Opinions of the Jurist.* New York: Dutton, 1916.

HUNT, WARD

Fairman, C. *Mr. Justice Miller and the Supreme Court, 1862–1890.* Cambridge: Harvard University Press, 1939.

"The Old Judge and the New: Mr. Justice Nelson and His Successor, Ward Hunt." 6 *Albany Law Journal* (July 1872–January 1873), pp. 400–401.

IREDELL, JAMES

Carson, H. L. "James Wilson and James Iredell: A Parallel and a Contrast." 7 *American Bar Association Journal* (March 1921), pp. 123–131.

Connor, H. G. "James Iredell: Lawyer, Statesman, Judge, 1751–1799." 60 *University of Pennsylvania Law Review* 225 (1911–1912).

Iredell, J. *The Papers of James Iredell.* Edited by D. Higginbotham. 2 vols. Raleigh, N.C.: Division of Archives and History, Department of Cultural Resources, 1976.

McRee, G. F., ed. *The Life and Correspondence of James Iredell.* Magnolia, Mass.: Peter Smith Publisher, 1949.

JACKSON, HOWELL E.

Doak, H. M. "Howell Edmunds Jackson." 1897 *Proceedings of the Bar Association of Tennessee* 76.

Memorial Proceedings. Washington, D.C.: Supreme Court, 159 U.S. 703 (1895).

JACKSON, ROBERT H.

Gerhart, E. C. *America's Advocate. Robert H. Jackson.* Indianapolis: Bobbs-Merrill, 1958.

Gerhart, E. C. *The Supreme Court in the American System of Government.* Cambridge: Harvard University Press, 1955.

Gerhart, E. C. *Supreme Court Justice Jackson: Lawyer's Judge.* Albany, N.Y.: "Q" Corp., 1961.

Schubert, G., ed. *Dispassionate Justice: A Synthesis of the Judicial Opinions of Robert H. Jackson.* Indianapolis: Bobbs-Merrill, 1969.

Seymour, W. N., P. Stewart, P. A. Freund, et al., eds. *Mr. Justice Jackson: Four Lectures in His Honor.* New York: Columbia University Press, 1969.

Steamer, R. J. *The Constitutional Doctrines of Mr. Justice Robert H. Jackson.* Ann Arbor, Mich.: University Microfilms International, 1981.

JAY, JOHN

Jay, W. *The Life of John Jay.* New York: Harper, 1833.

Johnston, H. P., ed. *The Correspondence and Public Papers of John Jay, 1763–1826.* New York: Putnam's, 1890, 1893.

Monaghan, F. *John Jay: Defender of Liberty.* New York: Bobbs-Merrill, 1935.

Morris, R. B. *John Jay, the Nation and the Court.* Boston. Boston University Press, 1967.

Morris, R. B., ed. *John Jay, the Making of a Revolutionary: Unpublished Papers, 1745–1780.* New York. Harper & Row, 1975.

JOHNSON, THOMAS

Delaplaine, E. S. *The Life of Thomas Johnson, Member of the Continental Congress, First Governor of the State of Maryland, and Associate Justice of the United States Supreme Court.* New York: F. H. Hitchcock, 1927.

JOHNSON, WILLIAM

Morgan, D. G. *Justice William Johnson, the First Dissenter: The Career and Constitutional Philosophy of a Jeffersonian Judge.* Columbia: University of South Carolina Press, 1954.

Morgan, D. G. "The Origin of Supreme Court Dissent." 10 *William and Mary Quarterly* 3 (July 1953), pp. 353–377.

Schroeder, O., Jr. "Life and Judicial Work of Justice William Johnson, Jr." 95 *University of Pennsylvania Law Review* 164 (1946–1947).

KENNEDY, ANTHONY M.

Kennedy, A. M. "The Constitution and the Spirit of Freedom." *The Gauer Distinguished Lecture in Law and Public Policy,* vol. 1. Washington, D. C.: National Legal Center for the Public Interest, 1990.

LAMAR, JOSEPH RUCKER

Lamar, C. P. *The Life of Joseph Rucker Lamar, 1857–1916.* New York: Putnam's, 1926.

Northen, W. J. "Men of Mark in Georgia." 4 *Atlanta* (1908).

LAMAR, LUCIUS Q. C.

Cate, W. A. *Lucius Q. C. Lamar: Secession and Reunion.* Chapel Hill: University of North Carolina Press, 1935.

Mayes, E. *Lucius Q. C. Lamar: His Life, Times and Speeches.* Nashville: Publishing House of the Methodist Episcopal Church, South, 1896.

Merrill, H. S. *Bourbon Leader.* Boston: Little, Brown, 1957.

Reeves, B. L. *Lucius Quintus Cincinnatus Lamar: Reluctant Secessionist and Spokesman for the South, 1860–1885.* Ann Arbor, Mich.: University Microfilms International, 1973.

LIVINGSTON, H. BROCKHOLST

Dunne, G. T. "The Story-Livingston Correspondence (1812–1822)." 10 *American Journal of Legal History* 3 (July 1966), pp. 224–236.

Livingston, E. B. *The Livingstons of Livingston Manor.* Knickerbocker, 1910.

LURTON, HORACE H.

Green, J. W. *Law and Lawyers: Sketches of the Federal Judges of Tennessee: Sketches of the Attorneys General of Tennessee.* Jackson, Tenn.: McCowat-Mercer Press, 1950.

Tucker, D. M. "Justice Horace Harmon Lurton: The Shaping of a National Progressive." 13 *American Journal of Legal History* 3 (July 1969), pp. 223–232.

Williams, S. C. "Judge Horace H. Lurton." 18 *Tennessee Law Review* (1944), pp. 242–250.

Wollman, H. "Justice Lurton's Will." 26 *Green Bag* (1914), p. 490.

MARSHALL, JOHN

Baker, L. *John Marshall: A Life in Law.* New York: Macmillan, 1974.

Beveridge, A. J. *The Life of John Marshall.* 4 vols. Boston: Houghton Mifflin, 1916.

Corwin, E. S. *John Marshall and the Constitution: A Chronicle of the Supreme Court.* New Haven: Yale University Press, 1921.

Cullen, C. T., and H. A. Johnson. *The Papers of John Marshall.* Chapel Hill: University of North Carolina Press, 1977.

Haskins, G. L., and H. A. Johnson. "Foundations of Power: John Marshall, 1801–1815." In *History of the Supreme Court of the United States.* New York: Macmillan, 1971.

Johnson, H. A., ed. *The Papers of John Marshall.* Vol. 1, *Correspondence and Papers, November 10, 1775–June 23, 1788.* Chapel Hill: University of North Carolina Press, 1974.

Jones, W. M., ed. *Chief Justice John Marshall: A Reappraisal.* Reprint. New York: Da Capo Press, 1971.

Marshall, J. *Papers of John Marshall.* 2 vols. Norman: University of Oklahoma Press, 1969.

Roche, J. P., ed. *John Marshall: Major Opinions and Other Writings.* Indianapolis: Bobbs-Merrill, 1966.

Servies, J. A. *A Bibliography of John Marshall.* Washington, D.C.: U.S. Commission for Celebration of 200th Anniversary of the Birth of John Marshall, 1956.

Severn, B. *John Marshall: The Man Who Made the Court Supreme.* New York: McKay, 1969.

Surrency, E., ed. *The Marshall Reader.* Dobbs Ferry, N.Y.: Oceana Publications, 1955.

Swindler, W. F. *The Constitution and Chief Justice Marshall.* New York: Dodd, Mead & Co., 1979.

MARSHALL, THURGOOD

"A Tribute to Justice Thurgood Marshall." 105 *Harvard Law Review* 23 (1991).

Bell, D. A. "An Epistolary Exploration for a Thurgood Marshall Biography." 6 *The Harvard Blackletter Journal* (Spring 1989), pp. 51–67.

Bland, R. W. *Private Pressure on Public Law: The Legal Career of Justice Thurgood Marshall.* Port Washington, N.Y.: Kennikat, 1973.

Fenderson, L. H. *Thurgood Marshall.* New York: McGraw-Hill, 1969.

"Justice Thurgood Marshall Symposium." 40 *Arkansas Law Review* 4 (1987).

"Tributes." 101 *Yale Law Journal* 1 (1991).

MATTHEWS, STANLEY

Chase, S. P. "Some Letters of Salmon P. Chase Written to Stanley Matthews." 34 *American Historical Review* 3 (April 1929), pp. 536–555.

Greoe, C. J. "Stanley Matthews." In W. D. Lewis, ed., *Seven Great American Lawyers.* Philadelphia: Lippincott, 1909.

McKENNA, JOSEPH

McDevitt, Brother M. B. *Joseph McKenna: Associate Justice of the United States.* Reprint. New York: Da Capo Press, 1974.

McKINLEY, JOHN

Hicks, J. "Associate Justice John McKinley: A Sketch." 18 *Alabama Law Review* 227 (1965).

McLEAN, JOHN

Weisenburger, F. P. *The Life of John McLean: A Politician on the United States Supreme Court.* Columbus: Ohio State University, 1937; New York: Da Capo Press, 1971.

McREYNOLDS, JAMES CLARK

Blaisdell, D. P. "Mr. Justice James Clark McReynolds." Thesis: University of Wisconsin, 1948.

Early, S. T., Jr. *James Clark McReynolds and the Judicial Process.* Ann Arbor, Mich.: University Microfilms International, 1982.

Gilberts, S. P. *James Clark McReynolds.* Privately published, 1946.

McCraw, J. B. "Justice James Clark McReynolds and the Supreme Court, 1914–1941." Thesis: University of Texas, Austin, 1949.

MILLER, SAMUEL F.

Barnes, W. H. *The Supreme Court of the United States.* Part II, *Barnes Illustrated Cyclopedia of the American Government,* 1875.

Fairman, C. *Mr. Justice Miller and the Supreme Court, 1862–1890.* Cambridge: Harvard University Press, 1939.

Gregory, C. N. *Samuel Freeman Miller.* Iowa City: State Historical Society of Iowa, 1907.

Miller, S. F. *Lectures on the Constitution.* New York, Albany: Banks & Bros., 1893.

MINTON, SHERMAN

Atkinson, D. N. "Opinion Writing on the Supreme Court, 1949–1956: The Views of Justice Sherman Minton." 49 *Temple Law Quarterly* 1 (Fall 1975), pp. 105–118.

"Papers of Sherman Minton." (Acquired by the Harry S Truman Library.)" 71 *American Historical Review* 4 (July 1966), p. 1540.

Wallace, H. L. "Mr. Justice Minton: Hoover Justice on the Supreme Court." 34 *Indiana Law Journal* 145 (1959).

MOODY, WILLIAM H.

Heffron, P. T. "Profile of a Public Man: William Moody." *Supreme Court Historical Society Yearbook 1980.* Washington, D.C.

Heffron, P. T. "Theodore Roosevelt and the Appointment of Mr. Justice Moody." 18 *Vanderbilt Law Review* 2 (March 1965), pp. 545–568.

Weiner, F. B. *The Life and Judicial Career of William Henry Moody.* Cambridge: Harvard University Press, 1937.

MOORE, ALFRED

Friedman, L. "Alfred Moore." *The Justices of the United States Supreme Court, 1789–1978, Their Lives and Major Opinions,* vol. 1. Edited by L. Friedman and F. L. Israel. New York: Chelsea House, 1980.

MURPHY, FRANK W.

Fine, S. *Frank Murphy: The Detroit Years.* Ann Arbor: University of Michigan Press, 1975.

Fine, S. *Frank Murphy: The New Deal Years.* Chicago: University of Chicago Press, 1979.

Frank, J. P. "Justice Murphy: The Goals Attempted." 59 *Yale Law Journal* (1949), pp. 1–26.

Howard, J. W., Jr. *Mr. Justice Murphy: A Political Biography.* Princeton: Princeton University Press, 1968.

Norris, H. *Mr. Justice Murphy and the Bill of Rights.* Dobbs Ferry, N.Y.: Oceana Publications, 1965.

NELSON, SAMUEL

Countryman, F. "Samuel Nelson." 19 *Green Bag* 329 (1927).

O'CONNOR, SANDRA DAY

Moore, R. H., Jr. "Justice O'Connor and the States." Paper presented at the annual meeting of the American Political Science Association, Birmingham, Alabama, November 3, 1983.

Shea, B. C. S. "Sandra Day O'Connor—Woman, Lawyer, Justice: Her First Four Terms on the Supreme Court." 55 *University of Missouri at Kansas City* (UMKC) Law Review 1 (Fall 1986), pp. 1–32.

PATERSON, WILLIAM

Degnan, D. A. "Justice William Paterson—Founder." 16 *Seton Hall Law Review* 2 (1986), pp. 313–338.

O'Connor, J. E. *William Paterson, Lawyer and Statesman, 1745–1806.* New Brunswick, N.J.: Rutgers University Press, 1979.

Warren, C. "New Light on the History of the Federal Judiciary Act of 1789." 37 *Harvard Law Review* 1 (November 1923), pp. 49–132.

Wood, G. S. *William Paterson of New Jersey, 1745–1806.* Fair Lawn, N.J.: Fair Lawn Press Inc., 1933.

PECKHAM, RUFUS W.

Duker, W. F. "Mr. Justice W. Peckham: The Police Power and the Individual in a Changing World." 47 *Brigham Young Law Review* (1980).

Hall, A. O. "Mr. Justice Peckham." 8 *Green Bag* (1896).

PITNEY, MAHLON

Breed, A. R. Thesis: "Mahlon Pitney." Princeton University, 1932.

"Mr. Justice Pitney." 24 *Green Bag* 211 (1912).

Stenzel, R. D. *An Approach to Individuality, Liberty and Equality: The Jurisprudence of Mr. Justice Pitney.* Ann Arbor, Mich.: University Microfilms International, 1982.

POWELL, LEWIS F., JR.

Freeman, G. C. "Justice Powell's Constitutional Opinions." 45 *Washington and Lee Law Review* 2 (Spring 1988), pp. 411–465.

Galloway, R. W. "Justice Lewis F. Powell, Jr." 28 *Santa Clara Law Review* 2 (Spring 1988), pp. 379–389.

"Hon. Lewis F. Powell, Jr." Symposium. *Richmond Law Review* (1977).

Kahn, P. W. "The Court, the Community, and the Judicial Balance: The Jurisprudence of Justice Powell." 97 *Yale Law Journal* 1 (November 1987), pp. 1–60.

Whitman, C. B. "Individual and Community: An Appreciation of Mr. Justice Powell." 68 *Virginia Law Review* 2 (1982), pp. 302–332.

Wilkinson III, J. H. *Serving Justice: A Supreme Court Clerk's View.* New York: Charterhouse, 1974.

REED, STANLEY F.

Fitzgerald, M. J. "Justice Reed: A Study of a Center Judge." Thesis: University of Chicago, 1950.

O'Brien, F. W. *Justice Reed and the First Amendment: The Religion Clauses.* Washington, D.C.: Georgetown University Press, 1958.

Prickett, M. D. S. "Stanley Forman Reed: Perspectives on a Judicial Epitaph." 8 *Hastings Constitutional Law Quarterly* 2 (Winter 1981), pp. 343–369.

REHNQUIST, WILLIAM H.

Davis, S. *Justice Rehnquist and the Constitution.* Princeton, N.J.: Princeton University Press, 1989.

Kleven, T. "The Constitutional Philosophy of Justice William H. Rehnquist." 8 *Vermont Law Review* 1 (Spring 1983).

Powell, J. "The Complete Jeffersonian: Justice Rehnquist and Federalism." 91 *Yale Law Journal* 7 (June 1982).

Rehnquist, W. H. "The Notion of a Living Constitution." 54 *Texas Law Review* 693 (1976).

Rehnquist, W. H. *The Supreme Court — How It Was — How It Is.* New York: William Morrow, 1987.

ROBERTS, OWEN J.

Leonard, C. A. *A Search for a Judicial Philosophy: Mr. Justice Roberts and the Constitutional Revolution of 1937.* Port Washington, N.Y.: Kennikat, 1971.

Pepper, G. W. "Owen J. Roberts: The Man." 104 *University of Pennsylvania Law Review* 3 (December 1955), pp. 372–379.

Roberts, O. J. *The Court and the Constitution.* Cambridge: Harvard University Press, 1951.

RUTLEDGE, JOHN

Barnwell, R. W. "Rutledge, 'The Dictator.'" 7 *Journal of Southern History* 215 (1941).

Barry, R. *Mr. Rutledge of South Carolina.* New York: Duell, Sloan and Pearce, 1942.

Flanders, H. *The Lives and Times of the Chief Justices of the Supreme Court of the United States.* Series: Classics in Legal History, vol. 2. Philadelphia: T. and J. W. Johnson, 1881; Buffalo: W. S. Hein, 1972.

Jones, F. R. "John Rutledge." 13 *Green Bag* 7 (July 1901), pp. 325–331.

RUTLEDGE, WILEY B.

Brant, I. "Mr. Justice Rutledge: The Man." 35 *Iowa Law Review* 4 (Summer 1950), pp. 544–565.

Harper, F. *Justice Rutledge and the Bright Constellation.* Indianapolis: Bobbs-Merrill, 1965.

Mosher, L. E. "Mr. Justice Rutledge's Philosophy of Civil Rights." 24 *New York University Law Quarterly* 4 (October 1949), pp. 661–706.

Rockwell, L. G. "Justice Rutledge on Civil Liberties." 59 *Yale Law Review* (1949), pp. 27–59.

Rutledge, W. B. *A Declaration of Legal Faith.* Lawrence: University Press of Kansas, 1947; New York: Da Capo Press, 1971.

"Wiley B. Rutledge." Symposium. *Iowa Law Review* (Summer 1950).

SANFORD, EDWARD T.

Cook, S. A. "Path to the High Bench: The Pre-Supreme Court Career of Justice Edward Terry Sanford." Thesis: University of Tennessee, 1977.

Sanford, E. T. *Blount College and the University of Tennessee.* Knoxville: University of Tennessee Press, 1894.

SCALIA, ANTONIN

Kannar, G. "The Constitutional Catechism of Antonin Scalia." 99 *Yale Law Journal* 6 (April 1990), pp. 1297–1357.

SHIRAS, GEORGE, JR.

Shiras III, G. *Justice George Shiras, Jr., of Pittsburgh: A Chronicle of His Family, Life, and Times.* Edited and completed by W. Shiras. Pittsburgh: University of Pittsburgh Press, 1953.

STEVENS, JOHN PAUL

Arledge, P. C. "John Paul Stevens: A Moderate Justice's Approach to Individual Rights." 10 *Whittier Law Review* 4 (1989), pp. 563–588.

Sickels, R. J. *John Paul Stevens and the Constitution: The Search for Balance.* University Park: Pennsylvania State University Press, 1988.

STEWART, POTTER

Barnett, H. M., and K. Levine. "Mr. Justice Stewart." 40 *New York University Law Review* 526 (1965).

Binion, G. N. *The Evolution of Constitutional Doctrine: The Role of Justice Stewart on a Changing Supreme Court.* Thesis: University of California, Los Angeles, 1977. Ann Arbor, Mich.: University Microfilms International, 1979.

Frank, J. B. *The Warren Court.* New York: Macmillan, 1964.

STONE, HARLAN FISKE

Kise, J. "The Constitutional Doctrines of Harlan Fiske Stone." Thesis: Harvard University, 1938.

Konefsky, S. J. *Chief Justice Stone and the Supreme Court.* New York: Macmillan, 1946.

Mason, A. T. *Harlan Fiske Stone: Pillar of the Law.* New York: Viking, 1956.

Stone, H. F. *Law and Its Administration.* New York: Columbia University Press, 1915.

Stone, L. H. "My Father the Chief Justice: Harlan F. Stone." *Supreme Court Historical Society Yearbook 1978.* Washington, D.C.

STORY, JOSEPH

Commager, H. S. "Joseph Story." In A. N. Holcombe et al., eds., *Gaspar G. Bacon Lectures on the Constitution of the United States.* Boston: Boston University, 1953.

Dunne, G. F. *Justice Joseph Story and the Rise of the Supreme Court.* New York: Simon & Schuster, 1970.

McClellan, J. *Joseph Story and the American Constitution: A Study in Political Legal Thought.* Norman: University of Oklahoma Press, 1971.

Schwartz, M. D., and J. C. Hogan. *Joseph Story: A Collection of Writings by an Eminent American Jurist.* Dobbs Ferry, N.Y.: Oceana Publications, 1959.

Story, J. *Commentaries on the Constitution of the United States.* Boston: C. C. Little & Brown, 1833.

Story, W. W. *Life and Letters of Joseph Story.* Edited by his son, W. W. Story. Boston: C. C. Little and J. Brown, 1851.

STRONG, WILLIAM

Fairman, C. *Mr. Justice Miller and the Supreme Court, 1862–1890.* Cambridge: Harvard University Press, 1939.

Obituary. *Philadelphia Public Ledger* (August 20, 1895).

SUTHERLAND, GEORGE

Mason, A. T. "The Conservative World of Mr. Justice Sutherland, 1883–1910." 32 *American Political Science Review* 3 (June 1938), pp. 443–477.

Paschal, J. F. *Mr. Justice Sutherland: A Man Against the State.* Princeton: Princeton University Press, 1951.

Sutherland, G. *Constitutional Power and World Affairs.* New York: Columbia University Press, 1919.

SWAYNE, NOAH H.

Silver, D. M. *Lincoln's Supreme Court.* Urbana: University of Illinois Press, 1956.

Swayne, N. W., comp. *The Descendants of Francis Swayne and Others.* Philadelphia: Lippincott, 1921.

TAFT, WILLIAM HOWARD

Anderson, J. I. *William Howard Taft: An Intimate History.* New York: Norton, 1981.

McHale, F. *President and Chief Justice: The Life and Public Services of William Howard Taft.* Philadelphia: Dorrance, 1931.

Mason, A. T. *William Howard Taft: Chief Justice.* New York: Simon & Schuster, 1965.

Pringle, H. F. *The Life and Times of William Howard Taft.* New York: Farrar & Rinehart, 1939.

Taft, W. H. *Liberty Under Law, an Interpretation of the Principles of Our Constitutional Government.* New Haven: Yale University Press, 1922.

Taft, W. H. *Our Chief Magistrate and His Powers.* New York: Columbia University Press, 1916.

TANEY, ROGER BROOKE

Lewis, W. *Without Fear or Favor: A Biography of Chief Justice Roger Brooke Taney.* Boston: Houghton Mifflin, 1965.

Palmer, B. W. *Marshall and Taney: Statesmen of the Law.* Minneapolis: University of Minnesota Press, 1939.

Smith, C. W., Jr. *Roger B. Taney: Jacksonian Jurist.* Chapel Hill: University of North Carolina Press, 1936; New York: Da Capo Press, 1973.

Steiner, B. C. *Life of Roger Brooke Taney, Chief Justice of the United States Supreme Court.* Baltimore: Williams & Wilkins, 1922.

Swisher, C. B. *Roger B. Taney.* Reprint. Hamden, Conn.: Archon Books, 1961.

Swisher, C. B. *The Taney Period, 1836–64.* New York: Macmillan, 1974.

Taylor, S. *Memoir of Roger Brooke Taney: Chief Justice of the Supreme Court of the United States.* Baltimore: J. Murphy & Co., 1872; New York: Da Capo Press, 1973.

THOMPSON, SMITH

Hammond, J. *The History of Political Parties in the State of New York.* Albany: 1842.

Roper, D. M. *Mr. Justice Thompson and the Constitution.* Thesis: Indiana University, 1963. Ann Arbor, Mich.: University Microfilms International, 1983.

TODD, THOMAS

"Letters of Judge Thomas Todd of Kentucky to His Son at College." 22 *William and Mary Quarterly* 20 (1913).

O'Rear, E. C. "Justice Thomas Todd." 38 *Register of the Kentucky State Historical Society* 113 (1940).

TRIMBLE, ROBERT

Goff, J. T. "Mr. Justice Trimble of the United States Supreme Court." 58 *Register of the Kentucky Historical Society* 6 (1960).

Schneider, A. N. "Robert Trimble: A Kentucky Justice on the Supreme Court." 12 *Kentucky State Bar Journal* 1 (December 1947), pp. 21–29.

VAN DEVANTER, WILLIS

Gould, L. L. *Willis Van Devanter in Wyoming Politics, 1884–1897.* Thesis: Yale University, 1966. Ann Arbor, Mich.: University Microfilms International, 1966.

Holsinger, M. P. "The Appointment of Supreme Court Justice Van Devanter: Study of Political Preferment." 12 *American Journal of Legal History* 4 (October 1968), pp. 324–335.

Holsinger, M. P. "Willis Van Devanter: Wyoming Leader, 1884–1897." 37 *Annals of Wyoming* 2 (October 1965), pp. 170–206.

Howard, J. O. B. "Constitutional Doctrines of Mr. Justice Van Devanter." Thesis: State University of Iowa, 1937.

VINSON, FRED M.

Bolner, J. "Chief Justice Vinson: A Study of His Politics and His Constitutional Law." Thesis: University of Virginia, 1962.

Frank, J. P. "Fred Vinson and the Chief Justiceship." 21 *University of Chicago Law Review* 212 (1954).

Hatcher, J. H. "The Education of the Thirteenth United States Chief Justice: Frederick Moore Vinson." 39 *West Virginia History* (1977/1978).

Hatcher, J. H. *Fred Vinson, Congressman from Kentucky: A Political Biography, 1890–1938.* Thesis: University of Cincinnati, 1967. Ann Arbor, Mich.: University Microfilms International, 1967.

Palmer, J. S. *The Vinson Court Era: The Supreme Court's Conference Votes: Data and Analysis. AMS Studies in Social History* No. 9. New York: AMS Press, 1990.

Pritchett, C. H. *Civil Liberties and the Vinson Court.* Chicago: University of Chicago Press, 1954.

WAITE, MORRISON R.

Magrath, C. P. "Chief Justice Waite and the 'Twin Relic': Reynolds v. United States." 18 *Vanderbilt Law Review* 507 (March 1965).

Magrath, C. P. *Morrison R. Waite: The Triumph of Character.* New York: Macmillan, 1963.

Morris, J. B. "Morrison Waite's Court." *Supreme Court Historical Society Yearbook 1980.* Washington, D.C.

Trimble, B. R. *Chief Justice Waite: Defender of the Public Interest.* Princeton: Princeton University Press, 1938.

WARREN, EARL

Christman, H. M., ed. *The Public Papers of Chief Justice Earl Warren.* New York: Simon & Schuster, 1959.

Katcher, L. *Earl Warren: A Political Biography.* New York: McGraw-Hill, 1967.

Pollack, J. H. *Earl Warren: The Judge Who Changed America.* Englewood Cliffs, N.J.: Prentice-Hall, 1979.

Schwartz, B. *Super Chief Earl Warren and His Supreme Court: A Judicial Biography.* New York: New York University Press, 1983.

Stone, I. *Earl Warren.* Englewood Cliffs, N.J.: Prentice-Hall, 1948.

Warren, E. *The Memoirs of Earl Warren.* New York: Doubleday, 1977.

Weaver, J. D. *Warren: The Man, the Court, the Era.* Boston: Little, Brown, 1967.

White, G. E. *Earl Warren: A Public Life.* New York: Oxford University Press, 1982.

WASHINGTON, BUSHROD

Annis, D. L. *Mr. Bushrod Washington, Supreme Court Justice on the Marshall Court.* Ann Arbor, Mich.: University Microfilms International, 1974.

Binney, R. *Bushrod Washington.* Sherman, 1858.

Washington, C. B. "Justice Bushrod Washington." 9 *Green Bag* 329 (1897).

WAYNE, JAMES M.

Lawrence, A. A. *James Moore Wayne: Southern Unionist.* Chapel Hill: University of North Carolina Press, 1943.

Livingston, J. "Honorable James M. Wayne of Georgia." 5 *United States Monthly Law Magazine* 382 (1852).

WHITE, BYRON R.

Armstrong, M. J. "A Barometer of Freedom: The Opinions of Mr. Justice White." 8 *Pepperdine Law Review* 1 pp. 157–187 (December 1980).

Mirabella, P. F. *Justice Byron R. White and Fundamental Freedoms.* Ann Arbor, Mich.: University Microfilms International, 1983.

"On the 25th Anniversary of His Accession [Justice Byron White] to the Supreme Court of the United States." Special Edition. 58 *University of Colorado Law Review* 3 (Summer 1987).

WHITE, EDWARD DOUGLASS

Hartman, H. F. "The Constitutional Doctrines of Edward Douglass White." Thesis: Cornell University, 1936. Ithaca, N.Y.: Cornell University Library, 1936.

Highsaw, R. B. *Edward Douglass White: Defender of Conservative Faith.* Baton Rouge: Louisiana State University, 1981.

Hill, A. B. "The Constitutional Doctrine of Chief Justice White." Thesis: University of California, 1981.

Klinkhamer, Sister M. C. *Edward Douglass White, Chief Justice of the United States.* Washington, D.C.: The Catholic University of America Press, 1948.

WHITTAKER, CHARLES E.

Douglas, W. O. "The Supreme Court Years of Charles Evans Whittaker." 40 *Texas Law Review* 6 (June 1962).

Volz, M. M. "A Biographical Sketch of Charles Evans Whittaker." 40 *Texas Law Review* 6 (June 1962).

Volz, M. M. "Mr. Justice Whittaker." 33 *Notre Dame Lawyer* 2 (March 1958), pp. 159–179.

WILSON, JAMES

Adams, R. G. *Selected Political Essays of James Wilson.* New York: 1930.

Konkle, B. A. *The Life and Writings of James Wilson, 1742–1798.* Vol. 2, *Letters.* Vol. 4, *American Political Science and Jurisprudence.* Philadelphia: The Presbyterian Historical Society, 1981. [Microfilm located at Friends Historical Library, Swarthmore College, Swarthmore, Penna.]

McCloskey, R. G., ed. *The Works of James Wilson.* Cambridge: Harvard University Press, 1967.

Seed, G. *James Wilson.* Millwood, N.Y.: KTO Press, 1978.

Smith, P. *James Wilson, Founding Father: 1742–1798.* Chapel Hill: University of North Carolina Press, 1956.

Wilson, J. *Commentaries on the Constitution of the United States.* Extracted from debates, published in Philadelphia by T. Lloyd, 1792.

WOODBURY, LEVI

Capowski, V. J. *The Making of a Jacksonian Democrat: Levi Woodbury, 1789–1831.* Thesis: Fordham University, 1966. Ann Arbor, Mich.: University Microfilms International, 1983.

Wheaton, P. D. *Levi Woodbury, Jacksonian Financier.* Thesis: University of Maryland, 1955. Ann Arbor, Mich.: University Microfilms International, 1977.

Woodbury, C. L., ed. *Writings of Levi Woodbury.* Boston: Little, Brown, 1852.

WOODS, WILLIAM B.

Baynes, T. E. "A Search of Justice Woods: Yankee from Georgia." *Supreme Court Historical Society Yearbook 1978.* Washington, D.C.

Proceedings of the Bench and Bar of the Supreme Court of the United States in Memoriam William B. Woods. 123 U.S. 761 (1887); 15 *Washington Law Reporter* 357 (1887).

SOURCES

The following were among the more important titles used in the research and writing of this book.

The foreword to this book is based on the following works: Joseph Alsop and Turner Catledge, *The 168 Days* (1938); Leonard Baker, *John Marshall: A Life in Law* (1974); Albert J. Beveridge, *The Life of John Marshall* (1919); William Garrott Brown, *The Life of Oliver Ellsworth* (1905); Jonathan Elliot, *The Debates in the Several State Conventions on the Adoption of the Federal Constitution, as Recommended by the General Convention at Philadelphia in 1787* (1891); Paul L. Ford, ed., *The Works of Thomas Jefferson* (1905); Felix Frankfurter and James M. Landis, *The Business of the Supreme Court: A Study in the Federal Judicial System* (1927); Paul A. Freund, ed., *The Oliver Wendell Holmes Devise: History of the Supreme Court of the United States* (vol. 1, Julius Goebel, Jr., 1971, and vol. 2, George L. Haskins and Herbert A. Johnson, 1981); Peter Dobkin Hall, *The Organization of American Culture, 1700-1900: Private Institutions, Elites, and the Origins of American Nationality* (1982); James Haw et al., *Stormy Patriot: The Life of Samuel Chase* (1980); William Jay, *The Life of John Jay* (1833); Maeva Marcus et al., eds., *The Documentary History of the Supreme Court of the United States, 1789-1800* (vol. 1, 1985, and vol. 2, 1988); Arthur M. Schlesinger, Jr., *The Age of Jackson* (1948); Joseph Story, *Commentaries on the Constitution of the United States* (Carolina Academic Press, ed., 1987); William F. Swindler, *The Constitution and Chief Justice Marshall* (1978); and Charles Warren, *The Supreme Court in United States History* (1935).

The biographical profiles in this book are based on entries in Leon Friedman and Fred L. Israel, eds., *The Justices of the United States Supreme Court, 1789-1978* (1980) and Congressional Quarterly, Inc., *Guide to the United States Supreme Court* (Elder Witt, ed., 1979). The description of the various meeting places of the Supreme Court is based on an entry in Congressional Quarterly, Inc., *The Supreme Court at Work* (Carolyn Goldinger, ed., 1990).

The bibliographies on the Supreme Court and the individual Justices were drawn from Albert P. Blaustein and Roy M. Mersky, *The First One Hundred Justices* (1978) and Facts on File Publications, *A Reference Guide to the United States Supreme Court* (Stephen P. Elliott, ed., 1986).

Commission on the Bicentennial of the United States Constitution

Warren E. Burger, *Chairman*
Frederick K. Biebel
Lindy Boggs
Herbert Brownell
Lynne V. Cheney
Philip M. Crane
Dennis DeConcini
William J. Green
Mark O. Hatfield
Edward Victor Hill

Damon J. Keith
Cornelia G. Kennedy
Edward M. Kennedy
Harry McKinley Lightsey, Jr.
Betty Southard Murphy
Thomas H. O'Connor
Phyllis Schlafly
Bernard H. Siegan
Obert C. Tanner
Strom Thurmond

Ronald H. Walker
Charles E. Wiggins
Charles Alan Wright

Former Commissioners
William Lucas
Edward P. Morgan (deceased)
Ted Stevens

Staff Director
Herbert M. Atherton

Acknowledgments

EDITORS
Don Reilly, Norman Murphy, Chuck Timanus

EDITORIAL CONSULTANT
Burnett Anderson

PROJECT MANAGER
Thomas J. Simon

DESIGNER
Donna Sicklesmith

PRODUCTION COORDINATOR
Patricia Andrews

**MANY ORGANIZATIONS AND INDIVIDUALS
CONTRIBUTED TO THIS PUBLICATION**

Herbert M. Atherton, J. Jackson Barlow, and Larry Ferezan; Shelly Dowling and the staff of the
Library of the Supreme Court of the United States; Gail Galloway, Lois Long, and the staff of the
Curator's Office of the Supreme Court of the United States; Supreme Court Historical Society;
George M. White and the staff of the Architect of the Capitol; U. S. Capitol Historical Society;
National Geographic Society; and the Government Printing Office.

PHOTO CREDITS

Portraits of the Chief and Associate Justices from the collection of the Supreme Court of the United States. With grateful appreciation to Vic Boswell, photographer.

Portraits of *Burger, Fortas,* and *Powell* by George Augusta. *Black* by John P. Black. *W. B. Rutledge* by Harold M. Brett. *Butler* and *Sutherland* by Nicholas Richard Brewer. *Brennan* by Paul C. Burns. *Salmon Chase* by William F. Cogswell. *Brandeis, Cardozo,* and *Sanford* by Eben F. Comins. *Frankfurter* and *Harlan (II)* by Gardner Cox. *Shiras* by A. L. Dahlberg. *Daniel* by Earl Clarke Daniel. *Vinson* by William Franklin Draper. *Byrnes* and *Minton* by Grace Annette Dupre. *Thompson* by Ashur B. Durand. *McReynolds* by Bjorn Egeli. *Miller* by Cornelia Adele Fassett. *Burton, Stone, Warren,* and *Whittaker* signed by C. J. Fox. *McKenna* by Edward Wilbur Dean Hamilton. *Stewart* by Ruth A. Nestor Hamilton. *Woods* by Erik Guide Haupt; *Campbell* by Haupt after Maurice Siegler. *Hunt, Taney,* and *Story* by George P. A. Healy; *Barbour* by Healy after Edward Peticolas. *Strong* by Robert Hinckley; *J. Rutledge* by Hinckley after John Trumbull. *Holmes* and *Reed* by Charles Sidney Hopkinson. *Taft* by Ernest Ludwig Ipsen. *Davis* by Jon M. Isaacs. *Brown* by Lewis Thomas Ives. *McLean* by John Wesley Jarvis. *R. Jackson* by John C. Johansen. *Roberts* by Alfred Jonniaux. *McKinley* and *Todd* by Matthew Harris Jouett. *Douglas* and *Murphy* by Elek Kanarek. *T. Marshall* by Simmi Knox. *Blair* by Ruth Koppang. *J. Lamar* and *L. Lamar* by Julian Lamar. *Pitney* and *Washington* by Adrian Lamb; *Blatchford* by Lamb after Daniel Huntington. *Goldberg* by Lucien LeBreton. *Brewer* by Robert Lea MacCameron. *Wayne* by John Maier. *Bradley* by Edmund Clarence Messer. *Grier* by Malcolm Stephens Parcell. *J. Marshall* by Rembrandt Peale. *Waite* by Israel Quick. *Field* and *E. White* by Albert Rosenthal; *Fuller* attributed to Rosenthal. *Clark, Gray, Lurton, Matthews, Moody, Peckham,* and *Swayne* by C. Gregory Stapko; *Catron* by Stapko after F. Girsch; *Iredell, Livingston, Moore,* and *Trimble* by Stapko after Albert Rosenthal; *Cushing* by Stapko after Max Rosenthal; *Paterson* by Stapko after James Sharples, Sr.; *Curtis* by Stapko after F. T. Stuart; *Jay* by Stapko after Gilbert Stuart. *Van Devanter* by Thomas E. Stephens. *Day* by Rolf Stoll. *Baldwin* by Thomas Sully. *Wilson* by Robert S. Susan. *H. Jackson* by Templeman. *Nelson* by Freeman Thorpe. *Hughes* by George Burroughs Torrey. *Clifford* by Joan Trimble-Smith. *Harlan (I)* by Pierre Troubetzkoy. *Ellsworth* by William R. Wheeler after Ralph Earl. *Samuel Chase* by Larry Dodd Wheeler after Charles Willson Peale; *Duvall* by Wheeler after Albert Rosenthal. *Clarke* by Edith Stevenson Wright. *T. Johnson, W. Johnson,* and *Woodbury* by unknown artists.

Photographs of *Blackmun, Kennedy, O'Connor, Rehnquist, Scalia, Souter, Stevens, Thomas,* and *B. White* © National Geographic Society.

Seal of the Supreme Court of the United States, courtesy of the Library of Congress. Seals of the States from a lithograph by A. J. Connell, courtesy of the Library of Congress.

From the Homes of the Court section: Photographs of the *Royal Exchange* (p. 242), *Old City Hall* (p. 243), *Construction of the Supreme Court* (p. 248), and *The Straight Bench* (p. 250), from the collection of the Supreme Court of the United States. Color lithograph of the *U.S. Capitol* (p. 244), courtesy of The Kiplinger Washington Collection. *Site on 204 B Street, Southeast* (p. 245) and *Old Senate Chambers* (p. 247), courtesy of the Library of Congress. *Supreme Court Chambers, U.S. Capitol* (p. 246), and *The Winged Bench* (p. 251) © Lee T. Anderson. *The Supreme Court* (p. 249) © Robert Llewllyn.

Sculpted marble panels from friezes by Adolph A. Weinman, located overhead, along all four sides of the Chamber of the Supreme Court. With grateful appreciation to Lee T. Anderson, photographer. *Majesty of the Law,* East wall (p. 4); *King John with Angel,* North wall (p. 6); *John Marshall and William Blackstone,* North wall (p. 8); *Liberty,* North wall (p. 240); *Justice and Divine Inspiration,* West wall (p. 252); and *Power of Government,* East wall (p. 282).

Marble backgrounds: Curtis Brightwater Marble, courtesy of Zellerbach Paper Company.